SHACKLETON WR977

DUTY CARRIED OUT

1957 – 1971

Compiled by
Robert Lindsay
and
Howard Heeley

Newark (Notts & Lincs) Air Museum Limited,
The Airfield, Winthorpe,
Newark, Notts, NG24 2NY

First Published 1995

ISBN 0 9500341 7 7

In admiration and memory of those who operated "10000 rivets flying loosely in close formation" for many long hours across the world's oceans.

Printed in England by Technical Print Services Ltd., Nottingham.

CONTENTS

ACKNOWLEDGEMENTS

Many thanks to all those who sent and helped to locate information for use in this book and kindly gave their permission for it to be used in this book. Thanks to those who also gave their valuable time to copying photo's, proof reading, etc.

Ashworth, R.C.B.
Ayling, J.
Buddin, T. (Flt.Lt.)
Carvell, R.
Cole, R.R.
Cole, P.S. (Sqdn.Ldr.)
Collins, D. (NAM)
Cook, D. (Gp.Capt.O.B.E.)
Davies, T.
Denham, J. (Sqdn.Ldr.)
Etkins, J. (Sqdn.Ldr.)
Goss, A.R. (Sqdn.Ldr.)
Goulding, B.
Greenwood, J. (Flt.Lt.)
Haig, T. (Sqdn.Ldr.)
Harman, G. (Flt.Lt.)
Head, M. (Wg.Cdr.)
Henderson, R.
Hickling, H. (Capt.)
Hosie, S., Mrs.
Houldsworth, M., Mrs.
Howard, P.J. (Flt.Lt.)
King, G.A. (Wg.Cdr.)
Kitching, C.
Langrish, R.
Lawrence, D. (Flt.Lt.)
Leggatt, D. (W/O)
Lindsay, K. (NAM)
Madden, B.
Madden, J.C. (Flt.Lt.)
Mallen, I.
Marston, P. (Sqdn.Ldr.)
Morris, P.
O'Brien, T. (cover design and illustrations)
Otter, A. (NAM)

Paterson, C. (Sqdn.Ldr.)
Pogson, R.
Proud, D.
Raybole, T.
Roberts, G.
Sage, G.
Shine, J.
Stephenson, S.
Wayne, R.M. (MAEOp)
Wayt, B.R. (Flt.Lt./Capt.)
White, D.B. (Wg.Cdr.)
Whittaker, P.
Wolff, J.
Woodward, B.
Zarraga, H.P. (Flt.Lt./Capt.)

Special thanks to the Shackleton Association and their members; contact via
Peter Dunn,
'Meadow View',
Perks Lane,
Prestwood,
Great Missenden,
Bucks.
HP16 0JH.

PREFACE

During Robert Lindsay's involvement with Newark Air Museum he has become 'WR977's Unofficial Historian', and an unashamed 'Shackleton Nut'. Whilst Robert's WR977 researches have always been very thorough and detailed, it was only whilst trying to confirm the Chichester sortie for a possible aviation print that the extent of her illustrious service career started to become apparent. Shortly after, the idea to record and publish these details in a book was conceived.

Throughout the research Robert has received many letters and a lot of information from members of the Shackleton Association around the world through contacts made in their magazine 'The Growler'. On behalf of Robert and my fellow Museum Directors, thank you all for helping to piece together the service details of the 'Old Grey Lady'.

Whilst every care has been taken to confirm all the details that follow, we recognise that some mistakes are inevitable. We welcome your comments, and if you are able to provide further sortie details we look forward to hearing from you.

When we embarked on this publishing project it was always intended to detail the Move and eventual Restoration of WR977. Unfortunately the vast amount of service details uncovered and ever pressing publishing deadlines forced us to suspend their inclusion. However it is intended that this will form the major part of a further book about WR977, which should be published next year all being well.

On a personal note I feel proud to have worked with Robert in putting together this book, albeit in the minor role of typist/editor and production advisor. Throughout the project Robert and I have worked closely together and with many, many different people. The only 'difficulty' I ever encountered was Robert's youthful modesty and expressed desire for anonymity regarding his involvement in the project. So Robert, when you see this Preface for the very first time i.e. when the book is printed, 'Well done, keep researching and SORRY for any embarrassment!'.

Howard Heeley, Secretary & Publicity Director
Newark Air Museum

WR977 on display at the Farnborough Airshow in September 1957, prior to her delivery to the RAF. (Museum Collection)

1

Birth of an Angel

Problems were encountered in the early stages of develpoment. The prototype Shackleton Mk.3 WR970 crashed in December 1956, narrowly missing the Derbyshire village of Foolow, killing four crew members. The main problem was stalling of the aerofoil, resulting in loss of control, and as with WR970, the aircraft to become inverted. Unfortunately this led to a more lengthy development programme. The problem was eventually resolved by fitting a 'v' plate on the inboard leading edge of the aerofoil, and better stall-warning devices including 'stick-shakers'.

The first production aircraft were for the South African Air Force. Eight aircraft having been ordered, the first two were handed over at Woodford in May 1957. The British aircraft built under contract 6403 (serials WR970-990, XF700-711 and XF730), were only a month behind the South African aircraft. The first production aircraft were used for further tests, the RAF receiving their first MR.3, WR976 at the end of August 1957.

Aircraft sections were built at Chadderton, Manchester before being moved a few miles to Woodford for assembly and test flying. Although we are unsure of the exact date, it is here that WR977 was assembled and flown for the first time. Whilst the date of her maiden flight is uncertain, WR977 was almost certainly well in to her flying programme by mid-August 1957. Several of these flights were carried out by Avro Chief Test-Pilot, Johnny Baker and Air Electronics Operator (AEO) Bob Pogson. The former already being well known for his Shackleton Mk.1 and Mk.2 test flights.

16.08.57: Bob Pogson records our first known flight for WR977 (although not necessarily the first!) from Woodford with J.D. Baker. Take off at 1620 hours, Landing at 1730 hours; Flight time 01.10 hours.

27.08.57: With the same crew as the previous flight, she took off at 1520 hours for a 1.50 hour flight landing back at 1710 hours.

12.09.57: This time with A. L. Blackman at the controls Bob Pogson logs an 1100 hours take off for a 0.55 hour flight, landing back again at 1155 hours.

In September 1957 A.V.Roe & Co. displayed WR977 in the static park of the SBAC Airshow at Farnborough. Whether any potential customers were attracted to the aircraft is uncertain.

Test flying resumed at Woodford soon after her return from Farnborough, with flights lasting around an hour each. By 13th September 1957 WR977 was ready for delivery to the RAF, destined to be 'taken on charge' (Authority 41G/C/1215) by 23 Maintenance Unit at Aldergrove, Northern Ireland. WR977 took off at 10.35am with A.L.Blackman at the controls. Arriving overhead Aldergrove a short time later they were unable to land due to undercarriage problems. WR977 was immediately returned to Woodford, touching down safely at 12.50pm. The problem was rectified and she was successfully delivered to 23 MU the following day, with a total of ten hours recorded on the airframe.

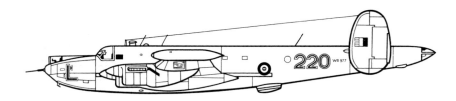

2

The Angel Gets Her Wings

22.09.57: On leaving 23 MU WR977 had flown just two hours since her delivery from the manufacturer. She was delivered to No. 220 Squadron under authority 41G/A/775 at RAF St.Eval, Cornwall, wearing the nose code 'L' (Lima), and painted in the overall dark sea-grey colour and scheme of the period. At 1235 hours at St.Eval she joined WR976, and in so doing became the RAF's second Mk.3 to enter operational service.

It was almost two weeks before her next recorded flight, although she had flown just over one hour since arriving on the squadron, possibly an "acceptance flight". For the next eight months, while accumulating one hundred and eighty six flying hours nothing is known of her duties.

.05.58: Having been without a Commanding Officer for the previous four months, No.220 Squadron was allocated a new Commanding Officer, Wing Commander J.G.Roberts. Soon after his arrival he took to the air for a brief familiarisation flight in WR979. He noted how much easier it was to fly the Mk.3 Shackleton despite the dramatic 14,000 lb weight increase over the earlier versions. Maxaret anti-lock braking on the new hydraulic systems, rather than the pneumatic systems of earlier Mk's of Shackleton was a great advantage. Wing Commander Roberts states,

> With those one could put the brakes on hard at touch-down and stop within five hundred yards. It was very impressive, but you had to make sure loose items in the aircraft were tied down, this could only be done with the Brake Emergency Air System selected.

09.06.58: This was his first operational sortie in WR977 with Flg.Off.Carter, taking her on a 6.15 hour flight to Woodford, Aldergrove and returning to St.Eval. This was her second flight after all Mk.3's had been grounded on May 3rd. It is believed that this was for micro-screw adjustment on the nose undercarriage leg, a fault having caused two aircraft, including WR976, to have nose-wheel failures on landing.

3

10-17.06.58: 58.32 hours of undetailed flying in four flights.

18.06.58: Wing Commander Roberts flew with Sqdn.Ldr.Haines and crew for an 8.15 hour NAVEX, completing a GCA and QGH.

By now 220 Squadron had their full complement of six Mk.3's, and was tasked to complete 'intensive flying trials' with the aircraft. Two false starts had been made before Wing Commander Roberts' arrival, and spares problems further delayed the start until sometime during June/July. Records show the squadron flew around one thousand hours in one month. Starting with local flights before working up to longer endurance flights with a full load of depth charges. (Information on these trials thanks to Chris Ashworth).

.06.58: Prior to her first three hundred hour minor service (at 306.00 Airframe Hours), it is believed that WR977 took part in the intensive flying trials, as she flew 111.35 hours during June, several sorties being over 10.00 hours long. This service grounded WR977 for most of July, but she returned to operations just before the trials were completed on August 6th.

28.07 - 22.08.58: 14 flights totalling 66.50 hours, but no further details.

.09.58: Saw the NATO exercises 'Shipshape' and 'Tallyho' begin. WR977 took part flying five sorties of 11.00 to 12.00 hours each during this period.

22.09.58: This sortie was flown by the Squadron Commander and Sqdn.Ldr.Patterson - a CLA exercise in the English Channel. 220 Squadron flew twenty two sorties of between 2.00 and 12.00 hours, with five 'mock' submarine kills, although it is unknown if any of these kills were recorded by WR977.

3

'Here (there) and everywhere'

During 1958 it had been decided to keep the famous Coastal Command squadron numbers, as Sunderland squadrons were being disbanded.

01.10.58: 220 Squadron was re-numbered 201 Squadron, moving their official base from RAF St.Eval to RAF St. Mawgan, the two being literally next door to each other. RAF St.Eval was closed soon after. WR977 retained the code 'L' and her existing colour scheme, with only the squadron number on the fuselage being altered to the new number.

To mark the occasion a full squadron photograph was taken and WR977 was chosen as the backdrop for the photograph. At this time it is interesting to note that the gun ports on the nose turret were fitted with provision for the Hispano cannon, although the guns themselves are not in evidence. The cannon had become available for fitment to the Mk.3's, having arrived at 220 squadron (now 201 squadron) earlier in the year.

In mid October after re-numbering, 201 Squadron went to Malta for 'Fair Isle' Exercises according to Chris Ashworth's book 'Avro's Maritime Heavyweight'. It ended on November 3rd and there is no firm proof that WR977 took part, although the pattern of daily flying hours indicate it may have, as she flew 40.00 hours in six sorties.

24.09. - 07.11.58: Nine undetailed flights totalling around 80.00 hours.

17.11.58: WR977 again had undercarriage problems, taking off from St.Mawgan again with Wing Commander Roberts at the controls, bound for Ballykelly in Northern Ireland. However as seemed to be very common on Mk.3's there was slight nose-wheel damage and the flight was aborted after only 0.30 hour, possibly connected with the fact that the nosewheels had been replaced on November 11th at 463.40 hours. After repairs were made she completed the 1.45 hour sortie later that day.

20.11.58 - 19.01.59: 16 undetailed flights totalling 100.00 hours.

Lima, WR977 taken on 01.10.58 during the Squadron re-numbering from 220 to 201.
(Museum Collection via M. Wells)

20.01.59: Wing Commander Roberts with Flg.Off.Carter flew 'Lima' for an Exercise 'Whitebait' sortie of 8.05 hours this involved an 'Air - Sea' search and 2.00 hours Instrument/cloud flying.

Later that month she completed several other long sorties of between 5.00 and 12.00 hours, but there is no firm evidence to indicate these flights were connected to the exercise. There is often little or no mention of 201 Squadron taking part in this exercise, it normally being attributed to 206 in the February.

22.01.59: 6.45 hour flight recorded but no further details.

26.01.59: Wing Commander Roberts flew with Sqdn.Ldr.Haines to Lossiemouth and return, a flight time of 5.35 hours.

27.01.59: A 2.25 hour sortie but with no details. After this flight her airframe hours had reached 588.50 and she was therefore due for a minor service, all four engines and all four rear props. were replaced.

14.03.59: WR977's first flight after her service, this was of 1.10 hour duration but further details are not known.

16.03. - 07.04.59: No details for 53.25 hours in eight flights.

08.04.59: Phil Whittaker provides details for this flight on which he flew as Signaller. Flt.Lt.Mannings was the pilot for the 6.10 hour Continuation training sortie. Take-off time was 1030 hours.

09.04. - 04.05.59: Seven flights totalling around 53.00 hours.

05.05.59: She flew an undetailed 9.40 hour sortie, after which No.1 engine was changed at 703.10 hours.

11.05.59: A 1.00 hour sortie brought her Airframe Hours to the 704.10 hour total noted when she was officially handed to A.V.Roe at Woodford under Authority 41/G/386.

14.05.59: This was a 1.25 hour flight, believed to be to Woodford for Phase 1 Mods.

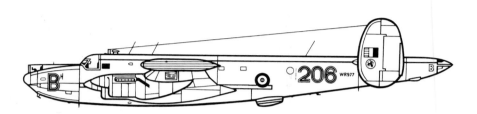

4

Phase 1 and 206 Squadron

Having returned to her 'birthplace' at Woodford she was to be updated to Phase 1 standard - the latest development for the Shackleton at that time. Phase 1 involved a whole series of modifications mainly concerning the avionics fit, the aim being to enhance the type's capabilities. New ASV (Air to Surface Vessel) Mk.21 radar replaced the ASV 13 fit. New navigation and radio equipment was also fitted as was an auto - pilot system, the Mk.3's having been without "GEORGE" until now. No significant external differences were apparent, despite the addition of a small ILS (Instrument Landing System) aerial beneath the bomb aimer's window.

The fact that WR977's Phase 1 modification took place at Woodford was somewhat unusual, as most other modifications occurred at 49 MU Colerne, Wilts. and a few at AVRO's at Langar, Notts. The only other Mk.3's to receive Phase 1 modification at Woodford were a few of the last production batch, but these were delivered as Phase 1 variants.

02.11.59: She once again met up with Bob Pogson on one of her test flights during the modification programme.He flew with O.J. Hawkins for a 55 minute flight from Wodford. Take off was at 1445 hours, and she landed at 1540 hours.

05.11.59: An undetailed 45 minute flight, probably another airtest.

10.11.59: On completion of modification WR977 was allocated to 206 squadron at St.Mawgan (Authority 41G/A/994) and was collected from Woodford by Flt.Lt.Peter Howard and crew. A 1.25 hour flight from Woodford back to St.Mawgan signalled the start of her second tour as the oldest MR.3 with the unit, this time coded 'B' and becoming only the third Phase 1 aircraft to operate with 206 squadron. It is believed she wore standard red and white squadron serial numbers and code letters, with red fuselage serials and a white top. The squadron emblem, for 206 an inverted octopus on a white disc, was also displayed at the bottom of the fins.

9

04.12.59: Flt.Lt.Fred Weaver flew as Co-Pilot to Flt.Lt.Clack for a 20 minute transit to Culdrose for torpedo trials in WR977. She decided to throw a hydraulic leak and consequently made a return transit to St. Mawgan without completing the trials.

08. - 15.12.59: Undetailed 21.50 hours flying.

16.12.59: Sqdn.Ldr.Spalding and Flt.Lt.Weaver flew a Stage II Exercise, Night Bombing and a NAVEX of 11.55 hours, including 1.30 hours of instrument flying.

31.12.59: This flight was a 'Stage II' bombing exercise. This is described by Flt.Lt. Bryn Wayt as

> an airborne anti - submarine exercise using a ground based simulator unit transmitting 'live' submarine underwater acoustic contact information and data.

Known crew members for this flight were: First pilot, Flt.Lt. Bill Houldsworth (noted Lancaster and Shackleton pilot who sadly passed away in 1991); Second pilot, Flt.Lt. Tony King; Navigators Flt.Lt.Jim Shine and Flt.Lt.Dave White; AEO Flt.Lt. 'Kit' Kitching. The last four crew members and Bill Houldsworth's widow were re - united with WR977 in December 1993 at the launch of the Newark Air Museum Shackleton print, 'Maltese Shackleton'.

5

206 SQUADRON & BEYOND - 'NOUGHT ESCAPES US'

05.01.60: This was a 'normal day/night trip' as Flt.Lt.Peter Howard describes it, flight duration just over 6.00 hours.

12. & 14.01.60: Undetailed flights almost 20 hours.

01.02.60: This flight was once again with Peter Howard, but they had to return to base (RTB) with a 'full rad deflection, or engine overheating on No. 3 engine after 3.45 hours'. After which a total of 61 hours take us to the 17th.

17.02.60: WR977 took part in Exercise Springex, 11.00 hours over the Bay of Biscay with Flt.Lt.Howard.

18.02. - 04.03.60: 28.15 hours undetailed.

16.03.60: This 'CASEX 44' sortie had to be cancelled due to a one hundred foot cloudbase, so a normal sortie of 8.00 hours was flown instead.

28. & 30.03.60: WR977 participated in Exercise Dawn Breeze V under the command of Flt.Lt.Howard, flying two sorties of 8.00 hours plus.

05. - 08.04.60: 25.00 hours undetailed.

12.04.60: WR977 had returned to Flt.Lt.Houldsworth and crew for a Tactical Navigation, Photography and Day Bombing sortie. At the end of the 8.30 hour sortie they were diverted to RAF Marham for an overnight stay. They returned to RAF St.Mawgan the next day after a 7.00 hour Stage II and Bombing Exercise.

19.04.60: Flt.Lt.'s Weaver and Aust flew '977 on Day Bombing, Radar Homings, SARAH Homings and Day & Night Mandatory 8.05 hours (4.30 hours of that at Night).

20.04.60: During this normal sortie, No.4 engine CSU went 'haywire' (as described in Flt.Lt.Howard's Log), and No.4's propellers had to be feathered. Five days later WR977 was officially taken in for a minor service at 1009 hours, a service due some twenty flying hours earlier.

21.04.60: Flt. Lt.Weaver records a further sortie with Flt.Lt.Aust on Day Bombing and an Airways Exercise of 7.25 hours Day and 1.50 hours Night.

22. & 25.04.60: 30.50 hours flown.

07.05.60: WR977 is recorded in three log books, Wing Commander David White, Flying Officer 'Kit' Kitching and John Madden as having been on SAR standby, and completing a 1.30 hour 'No.1 SAR Scramble' for a USAF C.121 on three engines. This flight is not recorded in the Daily Flying Hours Record for WR977. In addition some histories quote that she suffered a Category 3 accident at this time, requiring repair on site by AVRO. (N.B. Incident reports in the log book, verbal, written or official information have not been located to indicate that such an accident took place).

22.06.60: Officially back on-line, this was the same day that Flt.Lt.Houldsworth and crew returned from a three week detachment to Canada in XF730. WR977 flew for 2.45 hours.

24. & 28.06.60: 13.05 hours flown, no details.

30.06.60: WR977 completed a 15.00 hour Long Range Operational Flying Exercise, or 'L.R.O.F.E'. This included a Snort Simulation, Skid Bombing and a Practice SARAH (Search And Rescue And Homing Equipment), with 'Bill' Houldsworth at the controls. This was in fact his last flight in WR977, having recorded a total of thirty five hours in her.

04. & 07.07.60: 4.40 hours flown.

11.07.60: WR977 flew a display for the Royal Observer Corps in the hands of Flt.Lt.'s Weaver and Aust. 6.30 hours were flown on this sortie, whilst a total of 8.00 hours were recorded for the day.

13.07.60: Flt.Lt.'s Weaver and Aust, a NAVEX, T.A.C. Patrols & Night Bombing sortie flown, 10.30 hours, of which 1.30 hours were at night.

14.07.60: This next recorded flight was a 2.00 hour TORPEX (Torpedo Exercise) with Flt.Lt.Finan at the helm. The details for this and many other flights are thanks to Sqdn.Ldr.A.R.Goss, who was a Navigator on 206 Squadron during 1960 and 1961. Flt.Lt.Finan was a Canadian exchange officer at the time.

15.07.60: Flt.Lt.Weaver records a 5.20 hour Skid Bombing and Day Mandatory flight. A further 2.45 hours were flown according to the flight log.

20.07.60: Towards the end of July Bill Houldworth's former crew received a new captain, Sqdn.Ldr.Parry-Davies. This was his first recorded flight with WR977, a Torpedo Drop and mandatory Day/Night training sortie which lasted 8.40 hours.

28.07. & 04.08.60: 13.35 hours flown.

08.08.60: The Parry-Davies' crew flew a 5.10 hour Mandatory sortie. Sqdn.Ldr.Parry-Davies, Flt.Lt.King and crew completed a D.R. NAVEX (navigation exercise) and I.R.T. of over 16.00 hours.

12.08.60: Flt.Lt.Weaver flew as Co-Pilot to Flt.Lt.Aust for a Cat. Check and I.R.T. of 2.05 hours. A further short flight may have occurred around this time. She did not fly for a month after this date.

08.08.60: Flt.Lt.Aust and Weaver flew her on Exercise Fishplay V (see later) for 6.50 hours Day and 7.00 hours Night, for a total of 13.50 hours.

12.09.60: This was a particularly hectic day for WR977, albeit with conflicting data when comparing Log Book entries with the Daily Flying Hours Record, difficult discrepancies to resolve. Flt.Lt.Howard flew WR977 on two separate sorties, the first being Day Mandatory Training and I.R.T. of 2.25 hours and the second, Night Mandatory Training of 1.00 hours.

Sqdn.Ldr. Goss also records a 15.00 hour flight on WR977 (comprising of 9.50 hours day and 5.10 hours night) with Flt.Lt. Finan on Fishplay V, the build up to the long NATO exercise 'FALLEX 60' which was to further occupy WR977 later that month.

FALLEX 60 had begun in early September just off Norway, and gradually worked its way down over the Bay of Biscay to finish off Northern Spain. Exercise flights were flown out of many British bases and from Gibraltar. It was basically a large scale training exercise involving many squadrons, and entailed wing Shackletons performing most of their operational roles e.g. Anti-Submarine and Shipping Warfare, Shipping Protection etc. For the most part WR977 was used not only by 206 Squadron but by fellow St.Mawgan based unit 201 Squadron. This was possibly to help make up the numbers because they had three aircraft participating in the Farnborough Airshow.

14.09.60: Flt.Lt.'s Weaver and Aust, for a No Aids NAVEX of 9.30 hours.

21.09.60: A 13.00 hour undetailed sortie.

22.09.60: John Etkins (of Flt.Lt.Ostridge's crew, 201 Squadron) explains that Flt.Lt.Ostridge's crew was taken over by Wing Commander Stanbridge, the Officer Commanding Flying Wing St. Mawgan. WR977 was borrowed from 206 Squadron for this crew, and took to the air with them at 0620 hours for a 10.35 hour 'FALLEX Exercise'. Due to bad weather WR977 couldn't land at RAF St. Mawgan and diverted to RAF Ballykelly for an overnight stay.

23.09.60: 'At a more reasonable 0845 hours', as John Etkins puts it, WR977 took off for another FALLEX 60 Exercise of around 12.25 hours, returning to St.Mawgan on completion.

14

24.09.60: WR977 completed another 11.00 hour sortie, although there are no details of crew or the squadron.

26.09.60: WR977 returned to 206 Squadron and to Sqdn. Ldr. Parry-Davies' crew who flew her on a further 12.25 hour FALLEX sortie, according to log books taking off at 1735 hours. Possibly by this time 201 Squadron had received their aircraft back from Farnborough.

28.09.60: Wing Commander Stanbridge flew WR977 again with Parry-Davies and crew through a 12.00 hour FALLEX'60 sortie, taking off at 1040 hours.

During those seven days WR977 flew a total of 71.30 hours, FALLEX was said to be a complete success, although precise details of the success of WR977's sorties are not known.

04.10.60: WR977 flew an undetailed 7.40 hour flight.

07.10.60: Flt.Lt.Weaver flew WR977 with Flt.Lt.Aust for a Mandatory sortie which he records as a 2.30 hour sortie, however the aircraft log shows 5.05 hours, indicating a futher flight on this date.

07. - 19.10.60: Number 2 and 3 engine change at 1232.50 airframe hours.

19.10.60: Bravo flew an undetailed 1.50 hour flight, but it is most likely to have been an air test, or a flight cut short due to a fault, because after this she did not fly again until November 3rd whilst number 3 engine was replaced again.

03.11.60: Flt.Lt.Howard flew WR977 on a 1.15 hour air test, obviously after the engine change on October 19th. He also managed to pull in some Mandatory Training Circuits.

09.11.60: Flt.Lt.Weaver flew with Flt.Lt.Acklam and crew for a Day Bombing sortie and also did some formation flying for the 'Film Unit', the flight lasting 7.55 hours, with an hour instrument and cloud flying.

However a further flight took place on this date according to Alan Goss, when Flt.Lt.Finan completed a 2.30 hour Night Bombing sortie.

11.11.60: Flt.Lt.Weaver flew with Flt.Lt.Millman for a 5.05 hour No Aids Navigation Exercise and a Depth Charge Drop.

14. - 21.11.60: WR977 flew 18 hours in three flights, but no other details are known.

24.11.60: Flt.Lt.Howard again flew WR977 on Casex 44 and 43, taking approximately 4.25 hours.

05.12.60: An undetailed sortie of 6 hours in length.

06.12.60: Flt.Lt.Fred Weaver again flew with Flt.Lt.Millman for Bombing, a No Aids NAVEX and Mandatory Training, a flight lasting 8.30 hours.

08.12.60: WR977 returned to Parry-Davies and King for Radar Homings Cat. Bombing and Mandatory Training, with a take-off time of 0925 hours and the flight lasting 8 hours.

09.12.60: WR977 remained with part of the Parry-Davies crew, but Flt.Lt.Millman was Captain and First Pilot. Sqdn.Ldr.A.R.Goss flew as Navigator on this sortie too, along with Dave White, and so obviously replaced for this the usual Second Navigator for the crew. The sortie was a 'No Aids NAVEX' and some Mandatory Training - take off at 1050 hours and landing at 1645 hours.

12.12.60: Flt.Lt.Howard was about to complete a 'Normal Trip' when on returning to St.Mawgan the starboard main undercarriage green light did not show in the cockpit. The undercarriage was eventually locked down using the Emergency Air System, and a normal landing was made. Flight time 8.25 hours.

13 & 22.12.60: Two flights totalling 8.30 hours, no details.

22.12. - 02.01.61: Number 1 engine change at 1313.20 hours.

02.01.61: This was an Air Test after No.1 engine change. Flt.Lt. Howard was again at the controls for the 10 minute flight.

04.01.61: Flg.Off. 'Kit' Kitching made his last flight on WR977, having flown a total of 88 hours in her during the previous twelve months. Taking off at 1535 hours the Day Bombing and Mandatory Training Sortie, with 'Johnny' Madden, Dave White, Parry-Davies, Tony King and Thompson in the crew, lasted 1.25 hours Day and 3.15 hours Night.

16.01.61: 8.35 hours were recorded, no details available.

18.01.61: Flt.Lt.Howard again encountered problems when flying a CASEX 44 & 31 Sortie, and had to return to base with vibrations on No.3 engine, after 5.00 hours.

19.01.61: Fault rectified, Flt.Lt.Howard Air Tested WR977 for No.3 Engine, everything was satisfactory and she made a further 0.20 hour flight the next day.

20.01.61: This was a NAVEX lasting 5.20 hours, Navigator for the trip was Sqdn.Ldr.Goss. The sortie was the last on WR977 for Peter Howard, having completed almost 100 hours in her in just over one year. This was also WR977's last flight before her fourth minor service at 1337.20 hours, although the service was actually due at 1409.50 hours. WR977 did not fly again until February.

15.02.61: Records show a 0.50 hour flight, thought to be an air test.

17.02.61: 2.00 hours flown, no details.

21.02.61: Flt.Lt.Colman and Flt.Lt.Weaver flew an 11.10 hour 'LJX as briefed - Ocean Exercise', (Londonderry Joint Exercise, see JASSEX).

22.02.61: 9.20 hours were recorded, no details.

24.02.61: Is the next flight that has been traced, this is thanks to Alan Goss. Sqdn. Ldr. Thompson was the Captain for a 3.00 hour flight from Ballykelly to Langar and then on to St. Mawgan. However at least one flight is not recorded in this period, covering the trip to Ballykelly.

01.03.61: Records show a 10.00 hours flight, (5.00 hours Day and 5.00 hours Night), with Flt. Lt. Weaver and Flt. Lt. Colman for a FASTNEX, No Aids NAVEX and Bombing sortie, 30 minutes 'actual' instrument flying.

02.03.61: Sqdn. Ldr. Thompson flew a FASTNEX sortie lasting 10.20 hours.

06.03.61: Was a pilot conversion sortie flown by Flt. Lt. Aust, lasting 1.20 hours Day, take-off at 1150 hours.

10.03.61: A departure at 06.00 hours, saw the Officer Commanding 206 Squadron, Wing Commander J.E. Bazalgette fly WR977 with some of the Parry-Davies crew. The sortie was a Bombing Snort Simulation, use of SARAH and a simulated Lindholme Gear Drop, returning to St. Mawgan at 15.15 hours. (N.B. Lindholme Gear was survival equipment kept in three canisters, each connected by buoyant rope and dropped from the Bomb Bay).

21.03.61: 10.50 flying hours, no further details.

23.03.61: Flt. Lt. Colman and Flt. Lt. Weaver flew an 8.20 hour Day 'DAWN BREEZE' Exercise sortie.

27.03.61: Flt. Lt. Weaver, Flt. Lt. Leveridge and crew flew a 5.45 hour Day bombing, Radar Homing and SARAH sortie.
Later the same day Flt. Lt. Weaver flew two further sorties in WR977. First with Sqdn. Ldr. Thompson for 1.15 hours Categorisation Check, with 1.00 hour 'Simulated' instrument flying. He then flew with Flg. Off. Greenway for a 1.05 hour Day and Night Mandatory sortie. Total flying hours for the 27th was 8.05 hours.

18

06.04.61: 10.00 flying hours, no further details.

10.04.61: Sqdn.Ldr.Parry-Davies and crew, including 'Johnny' Madden completed a 'No Aids NAVEX' and Depth Charge Drop. This was Flg.Off.Colin Paterson's first flight in WR977, the flight also included Mandatory training and lasted 6.35 hours Day and 2.25 hours Night, with 30 minutes simulated Instrument flying.

12.04.61: Flt.Lt.Colman, Flt.Lt.Weaver and crew flew a Bombing, SARAH, Autolycus and Mandatory Training sortie which lasted 9.35 hours and included 1.30 hours 'actual Instrument flying'.

14.04.61: This was a busy day with WR977 making four separate sorties, with Sqdn.Ldr.Goss flying on three of them. First was a day CASEX lasting 05.10 hours with Flt.Lt.Finan as Captain and Flg.Off.Paterson. Flt.Lt.Finan also flew her on the second sortie from St. Mawgan to Langar, which lasted just over an hour. Flt. Lt.Bobart flew her back to St.Mawgan. Taking off at 1755 hours for an evening sortie was Flt.Lt.Bobart, a partly new crew and Wing Commander David White as Navigator. On the sortie they carried out SARAH Homings, Mandatory Training and Bombings lasting 03.30 hours and landed thirty minutes into the next day.

17.04.61: Flt.Lt.Colman, Flt.Lt.Weaver and crew flew WR977 for Snort Simulation, Night Bombing and SARAH. The flight lasted 5.05 hours Day and 2.00 hours Night.

19.04.61: Flt.Lt.Weaver and Sqdn.Ldr.Thompson completed a 10.10 hour flight in 'Bravo' for Patrols and Searches, Mandatory.

21.04.61: WR977 flew for 8.10 hours with Flt.Lt. Weaver and Flt.Lt.Colman on CASEX 41, and more Patrols and Bombing.

01.05.61: A 5.40 hour flight recorded after No.1 Rear Prop. change.

02.05.61: Alan Goss records that Flt.Lt.Finan flew her on a 12.00 hours FASTNEX sortie.

03. & 05.05.61: A total of 16.55 hours flown.

10.05.61: Sqdn.Ldr.Thompson, Flg.Off.Paterson with 'Johnny' Madden as Engineer and Dave White as Navigator, took off at 0225 hours to participate in Exercise 'Hallmark', the sortie lasted 9.40 hours.

12. - 25.05.61: Four flights were recorded for 41.50 hours, no further details.

29.05.61: Flt.Lt.Bobart and Flg.Off.Paterson flew her again with Dave White and John Madden in the crew. This time for a CASEX 41 and Night Mandatory Training, lasting 02.50 hours. Take-off at 2010 hours.

30.05.61 - 16.06.61: Number 2, 3 and 4 engines had their rear props changed.

16. - 29.06.61: No details for 26.55 hours in four flights.

03.07.61: Flg.Off.Paterson records 11.25 hours of CASEX 38,41 and 35 and a NAVEX with Flt.Lt.Lynn.

05 & 06.07.61: No details but 9.20 hours recorded.

11.07.61: Flt.Lt.Weaver records a 5.20 hour Bombing, Skids, Simulated Lindholme and Mandatory sortie with Flt.Lt.Colman, with 1.00 hour 'actual Instrument flying' included.

13.07.61: O.F.E., Bombing, SARAH Homings and Mandatory with Flt.Lt.Weaver and crew. The flight lasted 9.30 hours with 1.00 hours 'actual Instrument flying'.

13. - 19.07.61: No.1 engine change.

19.07.61: A 10 minute flight was recorded, no details but obviously a test flight after the engine change.

20.07.61: Flt.Lt.Colman and Flt.Lt.Weaver flew WR977 for night Mandatory circuits lasting 40 minutes. However 12.10 hours are recorded for that day, so a further 11.30 hour sortie may have taken place.

24.07.61: 7.25 hours flown, no further details.

25.07.61: Was a 07.10 hour Bombing sortie, flown with Flt.Lt. Finan as Captain. However a total of 8 airframe hours is shown indicating either a further short flight or a mistake in flying times.

14.08.61: Flt.Lt.Weaver and Flg.Off.Paterson flew WR977 for a No Aids NAVEX, Autolycus and Coding mission lasting 5.15 hours Day.

18.08.61: Saw WR977's first trip abroad for some time, when piloted by Flt.Lt.Millman she completed a 12.00 hour flight from St.Mawgan to Gibraltar.

22.08.61: Was the return flight from Gibraltar, WR977 recording a flight time of 06.30 hours.

22. - 28.08.61: No.4 engine change.

28.08. - 08.09.61: Four undetailed flights totalling 14.05 hours.

12.09.61: Flg.Off.Paterson and Flt.Lt.Weaver took WR977 from St.Mawgan to Oerland in Norway where they were on SAR Standby. Flight time was 7.45 hours, including 1.00 hour night flying.

15.09.61: WR977 and crew returned from Oerland, initially to Kinloss in 4.10 hours. Three hours of which were 'actual Instrument flying' They returned to St.Mawgan the same day in 3.30 hours, with a further 30 minutes instrument flying.

16.09.61: WR977 flew for 55 minutes undetailed, and was then grounded for her fifth minor service at 1717.35 hours and did not fly again until October 6th.

06. - 12.10.61: WR977 flew three sorties, for a total of 19.10 hours, no further details.

6

'SHAYA AMANZI'(Strike the Water)

Every year a Coastal Squadron was chosen to send a detachment of Shackletons to Cape Town, South Africa for joint exercises with the South African Air Force (S.A.A.F.), flying in conjunction with their Mk.3 Shackletons of 35 Squadron. In 1961 206 Squadron were selected to send three aircraft to D F Malan Airport, Cape Town for 'CAPEX'61'. WR977 'B' was chosen along with WR983 'D' and XF730 'C' to participate. The flight to Cape Town was led by Wing Commander J.E. Bazalgette in XF730, with Parry-Davies in WR983 and Finan in WR977. Details of the trip have been provided by four people who participated, Wing Commander David White, Squadron Leader Alan Goss, J.C.Madden and Gp.Capt.Doug Cook OBE.

Alan Goss's comments were as follows:

> Prior to our departure, the detachment were briefed by the AOC in C, Air Marshal Chilton on the political aspects of the visit. The tragedy of Sharpeville had just happened and the South Africans felt themselves to be friendless in the world. We were to avoid all discussion of the implications of Sharpeville, and we also learnt that a new South African Reformist Minister of Defence had closed all Service Mess Bars. However, in the light of our visit, special dispensation was given for their re-opening. This guaranteed the warmth of our welcome.

He continued,

> The services had also just become strictly bi-lingual, and we arrived during Afrikaans Month, when all orders and conversations had to be carried out in that language. But needless to say, all problems were overcome and it proved a very memorable visit.

Doug Cook had been attached to 206 Squadron from a ground tour at JASS (Joint Anti-Submarine School), to give some lectures in South Africa, he crewed with Parry-Davies in '983, and remembers:

> Navigating the length of Africa in those days was not easy. The only radio aid we had was a Radio Compass, and radio beacons were few and far between. The Squadron Navigator Leader had prepared packs of topographical maps for the route for each crew, but, again pin points were not easy to come by for much of the route. In Squadron Leader Parry-Davies' crew we adopted a routine whereby the three pilots rotated (I flew as third pilot) between the pilot seats and the nose gunner's position, with at least one pilot trying to keep track with the map. This team work along with the usual wizardry of the Navigators back at their table got us to Cape Town in good order.

19.10.61: The detachment's three aircraft took off from St.Mawgan at about 0400 hours. The first stage flight was of 08.45 hours duration, with everyone landing safely at El Adem for an overnight stay.

20.10.61: Another early departure at around 0300 hours, and the trio of Shackletons departed El Adem on a 10.25 hour flight to Khormaksar in Aden. Logs show WR977 flew for almost an hour longer than WR983, landing sometime between 1300 and 1400 hours.

21.10.61: Taking off a little later at 0500 hours, the trio's flight to Embakasi in Kenya took five hours. They stayed over until the 24th.

24.10.61: Departing Embakasi at between 0500 and 0600 hours, a flying time of 5.15 hours took the trio to Salisbury, Rhodesia, or as it is known today Harare, Zimbabwae. She had a Translation unit change on this date.

25.10.61: On this final stage of the journey, from Salisbury to D F Malan Airport in Cape Town, WR977 and her companion aircraft took off at 0600 hours and arrived safely in South Africa some six hours later. According to Doug Cook the aircraft overflew Fort Victoria, Johannesberg and Kimberley en route.

29.10.61: 'REX OF CAPEX '61' was planned for this date, and WR983 was scheduled to complete a 12.00 hour sortie. Having taken off at 2200 hours, Parry-Davies and crew had to return to base after forty five minutes with a fuel leak. Changing over to WR977 they departed again just after midnight, and went on to record 7.20 hours of night flying and 4.45 hours in daylight.

30.10.61: Sqdn.Ldr.Alan Goss recorded 0.50 hours of Mandatory Night Flight Training in WR977, with the Canadian exchange officer Flt.Lt.Finan.

31.10.61: Back with her allocated crew for the detachment, WR977 flew a 12.00 hour CAPEX'61 sortie. With WR983 undergoing repairs one

24

of her Navigators, Dave White flew with Wing Commander Bazalgette in XF730 for some missions.

02.11.61: 1.50 hour flight, but no further details.

06.11.61: Back to Flt.Lt.Finan for a 9.00 hour SARAH and Bombing sortie.

08.11.61: WR977 flew a further CAPEX mission with Flt.Lt.Finan of 12.10 hour duration.

09.11.61: Parry-Davies borrowed WR977 again and with Dave White and John Madden back in the crew flew a 10.05 hour sortie, take-off at 0930 hours. This involved Air to Air Photography, Tac. Ex., Skid Bombing and SARAH ops.

The return journey retraced the outward flight to Cape Town, with most take-offs being completed between 0400 and 0600 hours.

16.11.61: This was departure day, and a 6.00 hour flight from D F Malan to Salisbury.

17.11.61: Was a flight of almost 5.20 hours from Salisbury to Embakasi.

18.11.61: The leg to Khormaksar, Aden took 5.30 hours, and all crews had a day stopover as on the outward journey.

However due to engine problems WR983 and crew had to stay in Aden but Doug Cook had to return to JASS for his next course, so he re-crewed onto WR977 for the last leg to St.Mawgan.

20.11.61: Aden to El Adem, which took 9.30 hours.

Doug Cook recalls:

> As we climbed out of Aden I asked to go down to the nose and, fighting my way over piles of luggage, I settled in at the front.

21.11.61: The final stage from El Adem to St. Mawgan took 9.35 hours, with all aircraft arriving back in Cornwall between 1300 and 1400 hours local time. It is said that when they finally arrived each of the aircraft had suffered engine problems along the way. Records do not show specific problems for WR977. However more details are available for WR983.

Having missed the CAPEX exercises WR983 encountered further problems on the Embakasi to Khormaksar leg, and No.4 engine had to be feathered.

The return flight was Sqdn.Ldr.Goss's last flight in WR977, having recorded a total of 190 hours in her. CAPEX'61 was regarded as a success, but WR977 showed some scars, not flying again until December.

01.12.61: An early start at 0650 hours, with Wing Commander Bazalgette for a 10.00 hour CASEX 31 & 43 Day Bombing and Mandatory Sortie.

This was to be Wing Commander David White's last flight in WR977. He had flown 142.15 hours in her.

04. - 18.12.61: Four undetailed flights totalling 39.35 hours.

08.01.62: Flt.Lt.Weaver and Flg.Off.Paterson flew WR977 on Exercise 'Snowbound', a No Aids NAVEX and Bombing lasting 12.10 hours, including 6.35 hours night flying and 1.00 hour of simulated and actual instrument flying.

12.01.62: 7.00 hours recorded, no further details.

19.01.62: Details for this 5.15 hour sortie have been provided by the First Pilot Flt.Lt.Fred Weaver:

On the night of January 18th/19th, I and my crew (Colin Paterson was my Co-Pilot) were on SAR Standby Duty, when I was called to Station Operations and told that there was a sick seaman on a ship about 200 miles west of Brest who urgently needed life saving drugs. These were in glass containers and I was asked whether I thought I could deliver them ? Our aircraft was WR977.

The weather at St.Mawgan was very bad all night, but the forecast for the rendezvous area was quite reasonable. I suggested that the drugs be packed into a Lindholme container and that I should drop the complete Lindholme gear, which includes a self inflating dinghy containing a self activated light, which would be easier to find in the dark. I also requested that when the ship saw us it should heave to, and send a launch up wind of it, to which I would drop the drugs.

We located the M.V.Portland quite easily, it lit up its flying bridge on our approach. It was a very dark night and I never saw the outline of the ship or it's launch, only an intermittent pin prick of light which I assumed was a torch. I came down and dropped the survival equipment to it. If I remember rightly its limitation was that it had to be dropped at 130 knots at a height of 130 feet. The early Shackleton Mk.3's were fitted with a new British made Radio Altimeter which was often unserviceable and its readings unreliable, I therefore positioned a crew member in the nose to call out if he thought we were getting too close to the sea. (The Mk.3's have bomb door lights). In the event it was a perfect drop and as we left the area my Air Electronics Officer the late Flt.Lt. Joe Wagner said over the intercom. "If that was not a good advert for the Royal Air Force I do not know what is" We had a tricky landing back at St.Mawgan landing on the then existing short westerly runway in a gale with severe turbulence and downdraughts, low cloud and rain. After our landing, flying at the Station was cancelled because of the weather.

This was Flt.Lt.Weaver's last flight on WR977 on 206 Squadron, he had flown 207.35 hours in her.

26.01.62: Flt.Lt.Tony King was the Captain on this sortie, details of which have been provided by Flg.Off.Paterson. The sortie length was 1.15 hours.

Towards the end of January 1962, several squadron pilots, myself included, had not been able to complete our mandatory monthly training, particularly the requirement to complete three engine overshoots and landings; at this distance I forget the reason but it was probably a combination of other commitments and the limitations imposed by the weather conditions at that time of the year. On the 26th of the month, the weather was still proving unfriendly and, with a 300 foot cloudbase at St.Mawgan, the Flight Commanders decided that drastic action was needed if the dreaded 'squares' were not to remain unticked. The result was that about four or five pilots, together with a skeleton crew, were detailed that afternoon to take an aircraft (WR977) and proceed to RAF Thorney Island to complete the necessary training, Thorney being the nearest airfield with good enough weather. Tony King was nominated captain for the sortie and he and Harry Hickling occupied the two drivers' seats for the departure with the rest of us 'down the back'- I was seated in the galley area. Very shortly after we lifted off the runway, I remember feeling the unmistakable swing denoting a loss of power in one of the engines and sure enough one of the propellers was immediately feathered and we found ourselves climbing out through the murk on three engines. The low cloudbase meant that we could not achieve the necessary criteria for an assymetric return to St.Mawgan so there was no option but to continue to Thorney Island as planned. Of course the engine failure also meant that the projected programme of circuits and landings at Thorney was out of the question.

On arrival at Thorney Island, our disappointment at not having achieved what we had set out to do was somewhat tempered

by the thought that at least we should achieve an earlier arrival in the bar than we had been expecting. However we had reckoned without the determination of the aforementioned Flight Commanders back at base. On receiving the news of our problem on take-off, they had set about earning their vastly superior salaries by seeking another way to deny us an 'early bath'. It so happened that another squadron aircraft, captained by Dickie Bobart, had just completed a long sortie and had diverted to RAF Manston because of the bad weather at St.Mawgan. A hurried telephone call to Manston apparently just managed to catch Dickie before he and his crew disappeared on a well earned foray to the fleshpots of Ramsgate, and they were instructed to haul themselves and their serviceable Shack. down the coast to Thorney where we would take it over and complete our unfinished business. Unfortunately by the time they arrived, the foul weather which had hampered our efforts in Cornwall earlier in the day had tracked remorselessly eastwards and was now threatening to frustrate us once more. In the end, we just had time for Harry to fly one circuit and for the rest of us to claim that by being on board with him we had fulfilled our requirements too - well we had in spirit and it wasn't for the want of trying ! Which is why if you examine the Log Books of all the other pilots involved in this eventful escapade, you will find, I am sure, that we each completed our monthly training requirements in the same ten minutes we spent on board XF702 that dark and dismal evening at Thorney island. And we weren't too late getting to the bar after all !

This was Flg.Off.Paterson's last flight in WR977, he had flown some 75 hours in her. It was also 977's last flight on 206 Squadron, assuming the 28th was the Langar transit.

22.01.62: She flew an undetailed 8.10 hour sortie, and was officially logged as changed over from 206 Squadron to A.V.Roe, at 1925.05 hours under Authority MC/A/50 but was not taken until the 28th for 'RECON'. In some other written histories WR977 is recorded as having suffered a Category 4 accident on the 30th, repaired by AVRO although there is no Log Book evidence to support this. It has been suggested that it might have been salt water corrosion on the inner underside sections of wing, thus explaining the re-skinning.

One point which could not be tied in earlier, but is more than worth a mention is that John Madden, Engineer on the Houldsworth / Parry-Davies crew, was on 206 Squadron with his son Brian, who was an Aircraft Electrician. Brian flew many sorties as a supernumerary crew member in WR977, and they have many happy memories of her. One such incident cannot be definitely tied down to WR977 (but she seems to be the most probable aircraft) and it is certainly worth telling as they remember it:

My Dad is Engineer, I am supernumerary crew cooking in the galley, as an Aircraft Electrician, I recognise the smell of electrical burning. So, using Dad's old wartime helmet I report over the intercomm. Father's reaction is predictable, and I got my ears singed. But of course the burning was not in the galley, but just behind the Engineer's seat where a rather large HRC fuse was loose and vibrating, causing the Buzz to get nearly white hot, the subsequent fumes travelling along the starboard trunking into the galley.

Brian Madden was to meet WR977 again on her next Squadron when she had become a Phase 2.

7

PHASE 2 & THE RETURN TO 201 SQUADRON

The accident mentioned in the previous chapter is unconfirmed but would seem to have happened after her delivery to A.V.Roe at Langar in January 1992. Her delivery signalled the start of her Phase 2 modification programme, a further update to the Shackleton, and the addition of even more weight to the airframe.

Phase 2 modifications included: UHF Radio and UHF Radio Homer; Roof mounted HF radio posts were moved aft to a position almost over the fuselage side ditching exits; improved Radio Compass and TACAN (Tactical Air Navigation equipment). However the most noticeable and perhaps the most important change were the improved Mk.1C Sonic Sets and Orange Harvest ECM (Electronic Counter Measures) equipment. Their fitment led to a major external change which made the Phase 2 aircraft easily identifiable because of their roof mounted plinths and "Spark-plug" shaped aerials. Initial development problems with test aircraft delayed the programme but once under way each aircraft is believed to have taken around two months to complete.

This time was often longer if any rectification work had to be undertaken. The fact that WR977 took one year and two months to complete, suggests that some rectification work had to be undertaken and perhaps points to the aforementioned Cat.4 damage. The aircraft servicing log shows that she underwent RECON at 1926.35 hours, having arrived at Langar with 1925.00 hours on the airframe.

08.04.63: Sqdn.Ldr.Tom Haig remembers:

> We flew to Langar with Flt.Lt.Cyril Hannigan, but she wasn't ready so the company gave us a quick tour of the factory. We saw the first Phase III Shackleton on the jigs, she'd been stripped right back, even the paint taken off and the fuselage cut in the middle, pulled apart ready for about a six feet mid-section to be put in. They hosted us to lunch in what looked like the Manager's or Director's Dining Room.
>
> Since the aircraft wasn't airtested we waited for a Mk.2 coming through with Flt.Lt.Manning, (I'm not sure but I think he may have been going to Gibraltar, he could have been 42 Squadron), so we had a ride back in a Mk.2, and went back up the next day with Flt.Lt.Maycock.

09.04.63: Fully modified to Phase 2 standard, WR977 left Langar having only flown 7.10 hours since her arrival more than a year before. Having been officially transferred back in to St.Mawgan's under Authority MC/A/240 charge on April 5th, to re-join a former squadron, number 201, she actually departed Langar at 1605 hours with Flt.Lt.James as crew Captain. Transit 1.25 hours.

Tom Haig recalls

> This time we were looked after by the Canadians, who still had their Bristol Freighters - or as we used to call them 'Bristol Frighteners'. They took us down to their mess for lunch. WR977 still hadn't been airtested but the factory's Test Pilot flew in on a Devon (I think !). I seem to remember s guy in white overalls walking across from the Devon to the Shackleton, climbing aboard, off she went, some time later came back, landed, this bloke got out, signed Form 700, climbed back in his Devon and disappeared back to wherever he came from !
>
> That was the airtest done and we could now take her over and fly her back to St.Mawgan. It was like flying a new aeroplane, she'd only been in for a re-fit but everything was new or seemed new, with a smell of new paint, it was beautiful !

Another code letter change was made by the squadron, with WR977 becoming "O - Oscar". This partial identity change also reflected a new standard colour scheme for the time. Sqdn.Ldr.Mike Head says that the Squadron aircraft were distinguished by red tip tanks and light blue propeller bosses. Again she was the oldest MK3. on the squadron.

Sqdn.Ldr.Tom Haig provides the first 201 Squadron details, at the time he was a Flight Sergeant, and Signaller/AEO on the squadron.

11.04.63: A brief 1.15 hour flight out of St.Mawgan, before overseas travels again beckoned WR977.

12.04.63: Signaller Tom Haig notes

> We flew off to the States via the Azores. Wing Commander Rodney Roache flew with us, and he had a leg in plaster, so he sat with one leg on the rudder pedals and the other stuck down in the Bomb-Aimers passageway. I think he sat in the left hand seat with his right leg down in the passageway, and Flt.Lt.Frank James who had just become the Skipper of our crew - Mick Lawless was still the Captain - in the other seat and whenever Rodney wanted a bit of rudder when we were landing at Lajes, he would say something like 'A bit more right boot please Frank, a bit more right boot. That's enough thanks.' So Rodney flew onto the ground at the Azores with one foot on the pedals and Frank James supplying the other foot. Obviously, being the squadron C/O he does what he likes I suppose.

For this flight they left St.Mawgan at 1015 hours and flew for 6.40 hours.

13.04.63: Over to Tom Haig:

We went off on the next day, the 13th; what a date to fly to Brunswick, that's a 14.15 hour transit. While we'd been in Lajes we had met the crew of a Hastings. They'd been there for about a week, trying to get to Bermuda but they'd got 60 Knot headwinds and there was no way the Hastings was going to get there against such winds ! They were just sitting there waiting for the winds to change. But we were a bit more Northerly because we were to go up in a great circle and pass south of Canada and down in to Brunswick, and so we figured we'd be all right. So, off we went but we met headwinds as well, and at one stage we must have had a ground speed of about 90 Knots ! (Because the Mk.3 cruised at about 155 Knots.) Some aircraft were reporting to New York that they in fact had an hour less fuel than they would have to be airborne to get there ! So, in fact they were saying something like an estimate for the far bank of the pond 7 hours, fuel endurance 6 hours, which got New York quite excited. But we said hold on 'the winds might change', and obviously, I'm here today, the winds did change and no-one has heard of a 201 Squadron in its entirety going into the drink.

We could have diverted to Argencia in Canada, except that Rodney, on the radio said to those who had suggested the idea 'You will not, repeat not, divert'. The reason was that he knew the TV cameras were waiting for us to land at Brunswick because we were carrying a scroll from the Mayor of Plymouth, England, to the Mayor of Plymouth, Massachusettes, and I've a feeling we lost it, as it suddenly disappeared for a while. When we went into Brunswick we did our exercise, New Broom 11 and we did it in a storm, the weather was foul. But, it was a good trip and I managed to get down to New York, and it was quite successful. One of my first operational deployments for the Squadron, and I actually got one of the two submarines that the squadron claimed, so I was happy !

WR977 left Lajes at 0435 hours and arrived at Brunswick, Maine to participate in Exercise 'New Broom 11', a build up to 'Fishplay VII'. Two undetailed flights happened on April 16th and 17th, for a total of 15.05 hours flying time.

22.04.63: A late afternoon departure at 1720 hours, saw Flt.Lt. James and crew participate in a 15.00 hour (9.30 hour night) 'New Broom 11' close support sortie.

23.04.63: A short undetailed flight of 2.30 hours.

26.04.63: The return transit from Brunswick to Lajes was undertaken

Oscar, WR977 on the dispersal at Brunswick, Maine, during the Squadron detachment for Exercise New Broom - she is second from the right. WR977's Co-Pilot, David Sames is believed to be the person walking across the dispersal. (via Sqdn.Ldr.Tom Haig)

by Flt.Lt.James and crew. Take off was at 0730 hours and this stage took 10.10 hours, 1.30 hours at night.

> That was probably one of the coldest flights I ever made because some fool blocked up the heater intakes, so we couldn't use the heaters. Now on a night transit across the Atlantic with no heating it was bitter ! We kept the galley oven and hotplate on all the time, it was the only place we could get a bit of warmth, to thaw out. We actually sat in the galley with our feet in rubbish bags trying to insulate them, even with flying boots on it was bitterly cold. Not the most comfortable finish to a trip

27.04.63: Departing Lajes at 1003 hours. The flight lasted 8 hour day and 1.10 hours night. Sqdn.Ldr.Haig notes:

> We got back overhead St.Mawgan and the weather was foul, we tried a couple of times to get in, one or two made it, the third when he tried to get in went down with the GCA and found himself over the treble zoo crash gate, he slammed the power

Crew for the JASS course in 1963, who flew WR977 for the detachment.

Back Row from left to right: Flt.Sgt.Roy Hornby (1st Sig.); Sgt.Dave Bray (2nd Sig.); Sgt.Eric Meadous (3rd Sig.); Sgt.Tom Haig (4th Sig.); Sgt.Derek Hill (Flt.Eng.)

Front Row from left to right: Flt.Lt.Frank James (Capt.); Flt.Lt.Dave Sames (Co-Pilot); Flt.Lt.Arthur Brown (Nav.); Flt.Lt.Noel Montgomery RAAF (Nav.); Flg.Off.Mike Head (Nav.); Flg.Off.Colin Player (AEO).

on and went back into the murk when we decided that the GCA needed re-aligning, so all three of us diverted to Manston and spent the night there before we came back the next day.

29.04.63: WR977 departed Manston for the 2.00 hour transit back home to St.Mawgan at 1220 hours.

The following details have been provided by Wing Commander Mike Head, who described himself as being 'a junior navigator' on Rod Clayton's crew.

02.05.63: This was the date of his first flight on WR977 and Flt. Lt.Rod Clayton was Captain. They departed St.Mawgan at 1245 hours for a Stage II Skid-bombing and Mandatory Training sortie. Further details from Mike Head identifies the sortie as a demonstration of the Shackleton at three Army, Navy and Air Force Staff Colleges. Certain officers from the colleges are believed to have flown in WR977 during the demonstration. The flight lasted 07.35 hours, and he notes 'nothing special to report on this sortie'.

06. - 13.05.63: Four sorties totalling 26.15 hours, no details.

15.05.63: Tom Haig records a 4.40 hour Categorisation Board Flight, Night Tactics check with Flt.Lt.James. He says 'We all have to face the Trappers and we did it in '977'. Total for the day 11.15 hours.

21.05.63: 12.30 hours flown, no further details.

23.05.63: Flt.Lt.Clayton captained WR977 on a sortie lasting 08.30 hours, taking off at 0650 hours. This comprised CASEX, Skid-bombing, SARAH Homings, Radar trials and even a live Lindholme-gear drop. A further undetailed flight also occurred that day as the aircraft log records 12.15 hours flying.

04.06.63: This flight is recorded by Mike Head and Tom Haig, Flt.Lt.James captained WR977 on a 1.50 hour flight from St.Mawgan to Aldergrove, Northern Ireland, for a JASSEX (Joint Anti-Submarine School Exercise), take off was at 0725 hours.

Sqdn.Ldr.Haig:

That was us going to the annual JASS - Joint Submarine School - course at Londonderry, now called Ebrington Barracks, but in those days it was HMS Sea Eagle. We used to fly out of Ballykelly but we had to fly this one out of Aldergrove because Princess Margaret was at Bellykelly presenting Squadron Standards or something of the kind. So, we had a long trip right down to Aldergrove, Belfast before we could even fly.

10.06.63: Saw a 7.10 hour flight from Aldergrove with Flt.Lt. Clayton at the helm. This CASEX and day bombing sortie was a JASSEX build-up.

Two more flights occurred on June 11th and 12th, although no further details are available.

15.06.63: Taking off at noon, this 14.15 hour flight was a further JASSEX build-up sortie, on Surface Surveillance.

In early July Wing Commander P.G.South became the Commanding Officer of 201 Squadron.

16.06. - 14.07.63: No details for 61.50 hours. It is believed that at the end of a 10.50 hour trip on July 14th some fault occurred, as No.2 Engine was changed, and the flight on the 16th was a 15 minute air test, at 1535 hours. Mike Head suggests that with such a short flight

there must have been some calamity !.

17.06.63: After an 0845 hour departure, WR977 made a 1.15 hour flight to the Imperial Defence College at RAF Wittering for a 'display and delivery'. This is taken to mean that WR977 was on static display after an air display at the base. The return to St.Mawgan occurred at tea-time the following day, when a 1.20 hour flight was made at 1705 hours.

22.07.63: WR977 'O' completed a 4.35 hour afternoon sortie from 1350 hours, carrying out SIMTEX, Day Bombing and Mandatory Training, with Rod Clayton.

24.07.63: A total of 2.50 hours were flown. WR977 took off at 1000 hours bound for Wallasey. Unfortunately she went 'U/S.' (unserviceable) at Wallasey, number 3 engine had to be feathered forcing a return to St.Mawgan.

24.07. - 13.08.63: No.4 Engine changed.

13. - 21.08.63: 49.40 hours flown in five recorded flights, but no more details available.

23.08.63: Rod Clayton took off at 1415 hours and flew WR977 for 45 minutes on a dummy Lindholme gear drop.

27. - 30.08.63: Three flights for a total of 9.05 hours, no details.

03.09.63: This 4.15 hour flight with Rod Clayton and crew started at 0845 hours and was a practice for 'Exercise Unison'. This was an anti-submarine warfare demonstration for multi-national VIP's, which took place in Torbay. For the exercise sticks of six live depth charges were dropped from the aircraft on a designated target positioned between a destroyer and aircraft carrier stationed about 200 yards apart, and the submarine HMS Dreadnought, a similar distance away. (Details thanks to Chris Ashworth.)

An actual 'UNISON' exercise took place on the 4th with another aircraft carrying out the mission.

04.09.63: 14.20 hours recorded as flown, but with no further details. However she didn't fly again until September 10th due to a No.3 Engine change.

10.09.63: A further practice sortie was flown by WR977 at 0845 hours, and lasted 3.45 hours.

11.09.63: WR977 undertook the second live 'UNISON' exercise, at some time after 1000 hours with a flight duration of 2.55 hours. The drops were said to be very accurate and the whole event spectacular. The cascades of water produced by "Oscar's" depth charges were recorded in the log as 'quite a sight'.

12.09.63: 5.20 hours flown, but no further details.

13.09.63: After a break from '977, Tom Haig joined up with the aircraft again. An 0930 hour take-off with Flt.Lt.James as pilot, WR977 was scheduled to complete a SIMTEX, Skid-Bombing and Day Mandatory sortie. In the event the sortie only lasted 35 minutes, indicating some problems being encountered enroute. WR977 did not fly again until September 19th, when according to the aircraft's F.T. log she flew for 5 minutes, an indication of an air test after fault correction.

20.09.63: Flt.Lt.James and crew flew WR977 for a SAR Search, Autolycus, Bombing and Mandatory Training sortie, which lasted 5.00 hours, having left the runway at 0955 hours.

30.09.63: Flt.Lt.Frank James completed a 2.15 hour trip from St.Mawgan to Ballykelly leaving St.Mawgan at 0645 hours. The same pilot flew WR977 from Ballykelly on the 'Aird Whyte Competition'. Aird Whyte, consisted of two phases.

01.10.63: WR977 flown by Flt.Lt.James took part in the first phase, for 5.05 hours, taking off at 1410 hours.
>   Sqdn.Ldr.Haig:
>
>   So well had we done against the 'Trappers' that my crew was selected to be the Aird Whyte Competition Crew. Off we went to Ballykelly and we flew Phase 1, but we never flew Phase 2, we were disqualified. The reason being that we had to go out to an area of sea and look for a tame submarine, pick it up on radar, drop the sonar pattern on it, track it, carry out dummy attacks, with Di-Staff onboard watching what we were doing. We were the second to last crew to fly I think, and none of the other crews had found the tame submarine. The weather was foul, we went out and got a disappearing or fleeting contact just outside the area. 'Ah' said the Skipper, 'That's not inside the area, it's outside. A Di-Staff decision'. Di-Staff said 'Well looking at my orders here you've got to prosecute it'. So we prosecuted this attack, dropped Sonobouys on it - the old Mk.1C Sonics system wasn't a terribly serviceable piece of kit, valve technology and we actually used bouys that were recovered from the sea and re-conditioned. Such that they didn't work very successfully. We got what we thought was one active range and bearing on something, so we dropped more buoys, but nothing. We went back to Ballykelly, landed and we were told. 'At least you found something, nobody else has found anything, if the last aircraft doesn't you will be in the lead before we go onto Phase 2'.

The last crew, a 120 Squadron crew went off, and would you believe in that foul seas state the Flight Engineer of all people, the guy who doesn't normally look out of the window, he looked out of his little window and said 'Snort, starboard beam, mile and three quarters' or thereabouts! How he had spotted this none of us could figure out, but he had reported this Snort in a very high sea state, and sure enough it was the tame submarine and they carried out the necessary procedures. Back at Ballykelly afterwards a decision was made, they were in the lead, us, to get rid of any embarrassment, we were disqualified.

02.10.63: WR977 took off at 1500 hours and Sqdn.Ldr.Haig recalls:
The next day we flew off down the Irish Sea, 1.55 hours, the weather had improved, brightened up, a lovely day with a calm looking sea, not many waves breaking at all, and Frank James was sat up in the front on his 'Sun Lounge' thinking to himself 'Now if I was doing a submarine search today, what height would I fly at ? Probably where I am now, looking out I can see forever. Look at that wave breaking over there, my God that could be a Snort. Yep, I can see all round from here, a nice clear distinct horizon and there goes that wave again.' 'Captain to crew, Action Stations, Action Stations GO'. We swooped down and dropped some smoke markers on a submarine, which turned out to be a British submarine transitting to periscope depth. He acknowledged us and off we went.

02.10.63. Exercise submarine taken from WR977 by Flt.Sgt.Roy Hornby.
(via Sqdn.Ldr.Tom Haig)

04. & 09.10.63: No details covering two flights totalling 12.45 hours.

11.10.63: She left St.Mawgan at 0945 hours, with Wing Commander Bedford at the controls, flying a 9.15 hour sortie to Gibraltar, completing a DR NAVEX en route.

14.10.63: A 7.00 hour flight from 0945 hours, saw WR977 return to St.Mawgan.

17. & 21.10.63: Two flights recorded, no details. 7.20 hours.

22.10.63: Flt.Lt.James took-off at 1640 hours but returned to base in 1 hour, no further details available.

24.10.63: Saw Flt.Lt.James take her on a Stage II Skid-Bombing and Air Test at 0900 hours, suggesting the the R.T.B. on the 22nd was as a result of a fault. 4.20 hours flown.

After the October 24th flight WR977 was due for a 'minor' service at 2347.05 airframe hours, and did not fly again until December 6th.

11.10.63. 800 ton Coaster taken from the Beam position on WR977,
Wing Commander Bedford was Captain on this flight.

14.10.63. Gibraltar shortly after take-off,
WR977's starboard tail fin can be seen on the right hand edge of the picture.

14.10.63. Tarifa Point on the southern tip of Spain,
taken from Oscar during the transit back to the UK.

41

06.12.63. - 03.02.64: Fifteen flights totalling 100 hours, but no specific details.

03. - 12.02.64: No.1 Engine change.

12.02.64: Mike Head provides details of a 6.40 hour SIMTEX, SARAH homings and Skid Bombing sortie with Flt.Lt.Taylor, leaving the ground at 0950 hours.

13. - 26.02.64: Two flights totalling 9.25 hours, no details.

26.02.64: Tom Haig records a CASEX B3 A33/37 as briefed with Flt.Lt.James lasting 4.10 hours Day and 3.25 hours Night. Take-off was at 1450 hours.

28.02.64: An 8.00 hour flight recorded but no details. However she didn't fly again until March 7th due to a No.3 rear prop. change.

07.03.64: 10.25 hours recorded.

09.03.64: 19.30 hours recorded, of which Tom Haig records 9.50 hours as a Day/Night 'Magic Lantern' sortie, leaving the ground at 0010 hours with Flt.Lt.James. Sqdn.Ldr.Haig notes:

> Magic Lantern would be with the Navy, we were at Gibraltar at the time. I seem to remember it was an exercise in the western Med., in that narrow bit between Spain and North Africa.

10.03.64: Flt.Lt.James took off at 0750 hours and flew Oscar for 6.05 hours back from Gibraltar to St.Mawgan, No.2 front prop. changed.

14. - 17.03.64: Three sortie made, totalling 16.30 hours

18.03.64: Flt.Lt.James took off at 1020 hours for Stage II, Bombing and SHADEX for 7.50 hours. After this flight all four engines were changed at 2539.25 airframe hours. She didn't fly again until the next month.

8

'Shackleton or Sunderland, Sir ?'

During April 1964 WR977 was flown on a brief detachment, with Frank James as the 'official' captain and a 'H.R.O'(High-ranking RAF Officer), being taken along on his 'final jolly'. En route Mike Head and Tom Haig met up to fly as part of the same crew.

01.04.64: An undetailed 0.35 hour flight.

02.04.64: Tom Haig took to the air at 1030 hours in WR977 with Flt.Lt. James at the controls and the 'H.R.O.' as co-pilot. They departed St.Mawgan and set course for RAF Luqa, Malta, arriving 7.00 hours later for an overnight stay.

Sqdn.Ldr.Haig recalls:

> The H.R.O. wanted to go to Cyprus, because the Greeks and the Turks were shooting at each other and he wanted to see what things were like for himself. He said 'I want a Mark 3 Operational Crew' his Group tried to palm him off with a Mark 2, and he said something like 'Watch my lips, I want a Mark 3!'. So we flew out from St.Mawgan to Luqa.

03.04.64: They took off at 0830 hours for their next leg, a 5.35 hour journey to RAF Nicosia in Cyprus. They remained in Nicosia until the 6th, and it is here that Wing Commander Mike Head joined the crew. He had been in Cyprus since the February for a stint on 'Anti-Turkish Invasion Surveillance'.

Sqdn.Ldr.Haig:

> We did a night stop and flew on to Nicosia. I remember the H.R.O. saying to the Skipper, 'What are we doing way up here at 1500 feet Frank ?' 'Nothing special Sir, we were flight planned for it.' said Frank. 'Well what's wrong with fifty feet ?' asked our H.R.O. and Frank said 'Ah well if you're happy to go down to fifty feet, I'm happy to !'. So we did most of it at low level, sometimes down to fifty feet all the way across to Nicosia. I met an old friend of mine on the airfield at Luqa, who asked where we were going, I told him and he was going to the same place. He was in Transport Command and he said they would be at about 20,000 feet or thereabouts, I said 'We'll probably be at about 100 or 500', and he thought we were mad !

06.04.64: WR977 made a short 20 minute flight to RAF Akrotiri, having departed at 0600 hours. Mike Head has provided many 'interesting' details of the subsequent return flight, including the fact that WR977 was carrying something of obvious great importance to the 'H.R.O.' - the mast for his yacht !

Sqdn.Ldr.Haig:

From Nicosia we flew across to Akrotiri, that's where we had the photograph taken on the steps. We just flew across the Trudos Mountains, landed at Akrotiri, watched this exercise and then we went back to the U.K.

At 0900 hours WR977, her crew and a yachts mast left the runway at Akrotiri bound for RAF Luqa. Despite Flt.Lt.James being the official captain for the trip the 'H.R.O.' had a tendency to take over and Navigator Mike Head was asked to 'set course for a memory lane trip to Souda Bay in Crete'. From here on in the events are narrated by Mike Head's own recollections, by quoting from his jottings on the trip.

The 'H.R.O.' was famous for having 'sailed' an unserviceable Sunderland into the harbour (Souda Bay), using the rudder to steer, after a voyage of several days, only to discover that the base had been taken over in the meantime by those dreadful Germans. On that occasion he decided to stay there for the remainder of World War II.

This time he was determined to 'get his own back' by demonstrating his skills as a display pilot within the boundaries of the bay - despite the fact we had no communications with Souda and it was a Control Zone. We tried to persuade him it wasn't a good idea - the only response was a toothy grin and 'blame it on me if you have to'; he was enjoying himself ! That bit went OK (we weren't shot at - the Germans had gone). The worst was yet to come. Flying parallel to the coast, and therefore the East - West mountain range to the West of Crete, he decided to give us the benefit of his of his IMC landing/ditching technique in Sunderlands. This involved a gradual reduction in power to set up a 100 foot per minute decent and subsequent landing. A strong southerly wind was blowing over the mountains giving quite a downdraft where we were flying. The 'H.R.O.', wrapped up in his memories, momentarily forgot he was in a non-amphibious Mk.3 Shack., good old 'Oscar' (WR977). Frank James neatly took control and after a lot of noise, recovered from 50 feet AMSL (Above Mean Sea Level) or so !

Roy Hornby celebrated our continued 'dryness' by serving lunch, thereby getting the 'H.R.O.' into the galley or, more reluctantly, out of the cockpit ! Roy was, beyond doubt, very popular with both the 'H.R.O.' and the crew. His forte was cooking. Everywhere we went on the trip, he served a three course meal airborne based on the national dish of the nearest country, with silver service, white starched napkin and typed menu. I will never forget it !'

Sqdn.Ldr.Haig further notes:

That was the sortie, on the flight between Akrotiri and Luqa, we flew around the

Greek Islands, because the H.R.O. had been out there during the war on flying boats and he was telling his stories. He would tell them over the intercom, we would all listen and he would say 'Ah, yes the island coming up under the starboard wing, we used to anchor our boats in that bay down there, and the Germans would come over those hills and strafe us etc.

He bought a pannier load of citrus fruit, oranges and grapefruits. So before we took off we raided them, and Slim Hornby made a nice fruit salad. We had a menu printed for him in English, Greek and Turkish which he thought was rather sweet and he thought the fruit salads were quite delicious, 'You do wonderful things in that galley, Crew!'

As you will appreciate from this recollection, despite the annotation in Tom Haig's log book, that 'Oscar' was now at Newark Air Museum, she nearly did not make it that far ! But she landed safely at Luqa after 6.20 hours flying on the 6th.

06.04.64. WR977 on the ramp at RAF Akrotiri. (via Sqdn.Ldr.Tom Haig)

WR977 and crew at RAF Akrotiri. (via Sqdn.Ldr.Tom Haig)

08.04.64: The crew took to the air again at 1110 hours, from Luqa bound for Gibraltar.

Sqdn.Ldr.Haig:

> Once again from Luqa to Gibraltar we did the same thing, again we raided his fruit and he was delighted with the salad, and the menu was printed in English and Maltese, and the same again at Gibraltar only we did the menu in English and Spanish. On the way between Malta and Gibraltar he insisted on having a look at the beaches of the Balearic Islands, so we flew along the beaches of Majorca and Minorca, just to see them, a bit of nice weather. We flew level along the beaches and took the pretty route to Gib.

Further details are furnished by Mike Head:

> Frank James - ever mindful of the Souda Bay experience, was going around telling the crew that 'whatever else occurred, no way was the H.R.O. doing the landing at Gib !' (The runway at Gibraltar runs alongside the rock and extends right to the edge of the sea, and as we have already heard the H.R.O. apparently had no aversion to the Shackleton landing on water !)
>
> He even placed bets, putting his money where his mouth was. At five mile finals, landing to the west, he was fairly confident and was giving the thumbs-up sign to

46

all and sundry. The 'H.R.O.' was down the back and I was mildly concerned that I was going to lose my £1 wager. I needn't have worried ! At four miles to go (ages in a Shack.) the 'H.R.O.' shook himself, eased himself out of one of the beam seats, wandered forward, enquired of everyone's health and proceeded on towards the flight deck. At three miles to go, he motioned to the co-pilot to leave his seat; by two miles he was strapped in. At 1½ miles to go he announced 'I have control !' (he was half correct - Frank's hand never left the throttles). Down the back we all breathed audible sighs of relief - our money was safe... Frank was definitely "not a happy bear !"

Tom Haig also remembers that those on the ground said that it looked almost as if WR977 was descending into the airfield 'down a set of stairs', as one pilot put the power on and the other took it off again.

The landing at Gibraltar was successfully made after 6.15 hour flying, and they remained there until April 10th, when an apparently uneventful 7.40 hour flight taking off at 0820 hours was made home to St.Mawgan. The 'H.R.O.'s' final jolly was over, much to the relief of '977 and all of her crew.

Sqdn.Ldr.Haig:

When we got back to the U.K., just before we landed he said, 'By the way crew, I don't know if you're aware, but in th bomb-bay I've got some fruit in one of the panniers. I got it for a very reasonable price, if you're interested I'll let you have some, just pay the price I paid.' To which we all replied 'Many thanks Sir, but no thanks, no we've had enough citrus fruit on this trip.' He still doesn't know to this day I don't suppose, that we were nicking his fruit !

15.04.64: Sortie of 8.50 hours, no further details.

17.04.64: One week after the return from the eventful detachment to Cyprus Wing Commander Head again flew in WR977 with Flt.Lt. 'Duke' Wellington (RAAF). She took-off at 0855 hours for a 5.00 hour Skid Bombing, SIMTEX and Mandatory Training. WR977 flew a further 37 hours up until April 30th, this indicates a high standard of serviceability was enjoyed during this period. The tally for April 1964 was 85 hours, and this rate was maintained for several months.

01.05.64: Mike Head provides details of a TORPEX sortie which began at 0930 hours with Flt.Lt.Clayton as captain for 4.30 hours, once again it was an 'eventful' trip.

On May 1st '64, we did a live torpedo drop (back in my rightful crew under the captaincy of Flt.Lt.Rod Clayton in WR977) against a noise maker towed by a RAF

Launch. I guess it must have been a training Mk.30. These were designed to be submerged when running and then to float thereafter to aid recovery. This one decided to be different. First, it decided the launch should be the target (no decoy was going to fool this weapon !)

Secondly, bored with not being able to see, it decided to do the whole thing surfaced and, on a couple of occasions was damned near airborne. I cannot repeat here verbatim the message being broadcast to us by the crew of the launch, but they appeared to be somewhat concerned for their safety (they needn't have worried - the Squadron Weapons Officer was on board: surely he would know what to do...). The launch was subsequently declared repairable and the launch crew logged a dinghy drill.

07.05.64: 5.20 hours recorded, no details.

08.05.64: WR977 left the ground at 1255 hours with Flt.Lt.James for a Skid Bombing, SIMTEX and Mandatory sortie lasting 4.00 hours. A further flight of 7.00 hours must have been made on this date but no details are available.

08.-19.05.64: No.1 front prop change, and No.2 T.U.

19.05.64: Tom Haig logs a 2.20 hour transit with Sqdn.Ldr.Peasley taking off at 1245 hours. He notes:

Transit St.Mawgan - Ballykelly this was our next JASS course. We're flying from Ballykelly this time not Aldergrove, no Princess Margaret this year !

25.05. - 03.06.64: 24.40 hours flown in three flights but no further details.

04.06.64: Tom Haig logs an 0925 hour take-off for a 6.35 hour JASSEX with Flt.Lt.James.

07.06.64: A 9.50 hour sortie but with no details.

11.06.64: WR977 took-off at 0905 hours for a 13.40 hour sortie.
Tom Haig:

So just a straight standard JASS course except that we were delayed. 'Surveillance' - we all set out to come back and someone spotted a Russian R Class submarine in the JASS area so we all had to stay around and prosecute this target to

04.06.64. A British Leander class frigate taken from Oscar during JASSEX.

exhaustion, which we did, we got exhausted !! He eventually surfaced and tootled away, as he had every right to do, after all it is an International waterway. In the meantime we all got delayed in Northern Ireland.

13. - 18.06.64: 24.35 hours flown in total.

20.06.64: Mike Head records a 1.40 hour flight with Flt.Lt.Clayton completing Air Displays over Exeter and Bristol in the late afternoon, before returning to St.Mawgan. She took off at 1515 hours so she was obviously fairly late in the display programme.

20. - 25.06.64: No.3 front prop. change.

25.06.64: 5.05 hours, no details.

In July Wing Commander Mike Head and crew plus Tom Haig's Crew did a stint of intensive flying in 977, indeed Mike Head refers to it as an 'epic

49

Co-Pilot Dave Sames in the left hand seat.

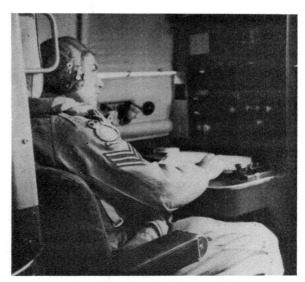

Signaller Sgt.Bryn Fieldhouse on W/T.

50

Flight Engineer Derek Hill.

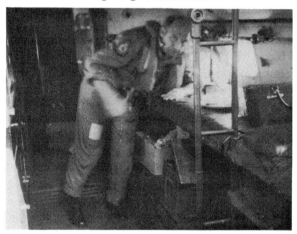

Crew Captain and Pilot Flt.Lt.Frank James, who was on a diet and is seen here snaffling a piece of cheese from the galley, (quoting from the reverse side of the photograph 'Note blurred right hand and look of guilt!'

Footnote: These four photographs came via Sqdn.Ldr.Tom Haig. By process of elimination it is believed these were taken on WR977. The condition of the interior suggests that the aircraft had been re-conditioned, as WR977 had. Tom Haig has also established they were taken between May and July 1964, a particularly active period from Oscar, WR977.

week'. They were flying from Kinloss to conduct a trial with a submarine some eight hours or so North, during the formative years of what was to become 'Sub-Air'. All hours were logged as day flying as internal lighting was never used. Mike Head's crew for the trip was as follows: Captain - Flt.Lt. Rod Clayton; Co-pilot - Ivor Gibbs; 1st Nav. - Jim Fahey; 2nd Nav. - Mike Head; AEO - Dick Tuson; Engineer - Wally Boreham; Communications, Aircraft Recce., Radar and Galley Slave 'Extraordinaire' - Mick Muttit; Wally Heaton: Al (for F++++'s sake) Miller and Stan Mathews.

03.07.64: Rod Clayton's crew were airborne at 0350 hours for a 17.00 hour day sortie, these were Sub-Air trials, as later explained by Sqdn.Ldr Haig.

05.07.64: Airborne at 0925 hours for a 19.10 hour sortie, with Rod Clayton, Mike Head and Crew.

09.07.64: Mike Head's Crew took off at 2040 hours for a 20 hour flight. A total of 56 hours were flown in three sorties over six days by Mike Head. In between the sorties Mike Head was teaching an Australian to play tennis! Needless to say he was pretty tired.

13.09.64: 16.35 hours recorded, no details.

16.09.64: WR977 took off at 1455 hours with Flt.Lt.James at the controls for 'OPERATION ADJUTANT' which lasted 18.05 hours.
Sqdn.Ldr.Haig:

> Look at the length of those trips, 18.05 hours. We were flying from Kinloss to Bear island and doing a Sub-Air just south of Bear Island. We couldn't do it out of Norway because we were up to our limit of U.K. airframes on the ground in Norway due to the political situation, so we had to fly from Kinloss which meant a 7 hour transit up to task, 4 hours on task and then 7 hours back. When we got up there an 'O' Class British Submarine was there, her job was to lay deep and silent and watch the Russian exercise, and listen to contacts coming through. Every so often she would pop up, speak to the aircraft on station, give us all her contacts and then we would go around and see what they were. Strange old sorties though, because you would be half way to your patrol area, or just over half way when you would hear your relief getting airborne behind you. So while you were still in transit to the area, your relief was already on its way.

They were also quite tiring trips, and infact those were the trips where I took photographs by the midnight sun. To do a trip like that, if I can take you through it, I can remember leaving the Sergeant's Mess, had a lime and lemon in the bar, put my glass down, went off and got ready to go down to Briefing, briefed for the trip, went out, got airborne, landed back, went to de-brief, went back to the Mess. I walked into the bar at the same time the following night and ordered a pint. That had been my 24 hours, that was it gone. The people who I'd left on the Friday night or whatever it was, they had a night in the bar, a good nights sleep, the following day they'd got up, gone into town, done a bit of shopping, come back had lunch, gone to bed and had a nap after lunch, had a good old shower, got dressed, all spruced up, when this smelly hairy looking thing walked in and ordered a pint. That was me who had left them the previous evening ! But this was pretty standard for all of us, you got pretty sweaty on those trips.

Infact one bloke, a new lad on the Squadron, Hugh Stewart, spent about three weeks on the Squadron and was then ordered to take two weeks leave, because he had transferred from crew to crew in order to stay up at Kinloss where his fiancee was. This meant he could stay in his home town and see his girlfriend when he wasn't flying, and with his wedding coming up in the near future he was quite happy to do these trips. by the time he had been on the Squadron a month he had exceeded his flying hours.

19.07.64: 18.05 hours recorded, no details, but the sortie length and the time span of the exercise indicate that it was most likely another Adjutant sortie.

Chris Ashworth notes on Operation Adjutant 'by the time the experiment was concluded on August 8th, 2027 hours had been flown in several sorties.' As we have seen WR977 took part in several 18.00 hour plus sorties.

21. & 23.07.64: 4.05 hours no details.

23.07. - 19.08.64: No.1 & 3 Engines and 1, 3 & 4TU's, No.2 & 4 rear props and No.4 front prop. changed. A 0.50 hour flight on the 19th was presumably an airtest after those changes.

19.08. - 15.09.64: No details in 8 flights totalling 68.00 hours.

20.09.64: This was to be Mike Head's last flight in 'Oscar'. Taking off at 0930 hours for a SURVEX sortie which lasted 11.55 hours, 1.25 hours of which were at night.

Wing Commander Head had flown 157 hours in WR977 in a period of 16 months, 56 hours being during the 'epic' week in July 1964. He has worked this out to about 17% of his flying time in that period, indicating an 'on-line' Squadron Inventory of around six aircraft available per day, which he says, 'seems about right'.

23.08. - 30.09.64: 55 hours flown in five sorties.

01.10.64: WR977 flew on Exercise 'Team Work', after taking off at 0050 hours she flew 5.35 hours night and 6.00 hours day. Details of the exercise are not available, but Sqdn.Ldr.Haig notes that Flt.Lt.John Reddish had taken over as crew Captain.

In his book R.C.B Ashworth notes that 'Operation Darwin' was aimed at locating and shadowing the Russian Northern and Baltic Fleets, which were gathering in anticipation of the start of NATO Exercise Teamwork on September 27th.

02. & 12.10.64: Two sorties flown for 28.10 hours, with no details. After which No.'s 1 & 3 engines were changed.

15. - 21.10.64: 37.15 hours flown in three sorties.

26.10.64: Flt.Lt.Reddish and his crew took off at 1730 hours and flew a Stage II, Skid Bombing and Mandatory flight, 0.30 hour day and 4.55 hours night. However a further flight must have taken place as the total flying time was 10.25 hours for the 26th.

28. - 30.10.64: Three sorties flown, a total of 13.25 hours. After the 30th she didn't fly for over ten days as No.3 rear prop. was changed at 3075.15 airframe hours.

11.11.64: Sqdn.Ldr.Haig provides details of the sorties on this date:
Airways St.Mawgan to Renfrew, Airways Renfrew to St.Mawgan. That was a trip to the Rolls Royce factory at Hillingdon for the crew. I went up with them, and said 'Look, I'm not all that bothered about going round the factory, can I go and have a cup of tea with my Mum ?' So I did, I took the bus home and had a cup of tea with my Mother and Father, who were quite surprised to see me arrive in uniform.

I went back to Renfrew, which was Glasgow Airport at the time, now defunct, walked into the Restaurant/Cafeteria and said 'Could I have a large pot of boiling water please ?' Which they gave me, I took it out to the aircraft, poured it into the water boiler, gave them back the empty pot. As soon as we were airborne I had a cup of tea ready, which amazed the crew because I had done it so quickly, having had boiled water !!!

The trip there lasted 2.40 hours, all day flying leaving St.Mawgan at 0850 hours and the trip back at 1630 hours lasted 0.50 hours day and 1.30 hours night, for a daily total of 5 hours.

19. - 25.11.64: 21.20 hours flown in three sorties.

26.11.64: Flt.Lt.Reddish and crew flew a 5.50 hour SAR, 1.25 of which was at night. They took off at 1205 hours.

27.11.64: With Flt.Lt.Reddish and crew she left the runway at 1000 hours and flew a 3.50 hour SIMTEX and Skid Bombing sortie, but as the total flying time was 7.10 hours a further flight must have taken place.

30.11. - 21.12.64: A total of 11 sorties flown making a total of 71.35 hours, but with no details. After this No.2 rear prop. and No.'s 2 and 4 engines were changed.

30.12.64. - 06.01.65: Four sorties for a total of 25.00 hours.

07.01.65: Sqdn.Ldr.Haig records a L.R.O.F.E., C.R. Bombing, Photography and ECM flight, which lasted 7.00 hour day and 5.10 hours night. Take off time was 1000 hours.

08.01.65: Obviously '977 must have flown to Kinloss the previous day for an overnight stay, as Flt.Lt.Reddish and crew flew back from there to St.Mawgan taking off at 0940 hours, flight time 3.20 hours.

11.01.65: '977 flew an 11.00 hour exercise Tightlines sortie but no details of the Exercise are available, this was flown by Flt.Lt.Reddish, Tom Haig and crew taking off at 0610 hours.

11.1.65. A 1200 Ton Coaster, photographed from WR977 by Flt.Lt.Reddish and crew.

13. & 14.01.65: 17.45 hours flown. No.4 engine, T.U. and front and rear props. were changed at 3252.55 airframe hours. A 30 minute flight on the 25th suggests a test flight.

26.01.65: Flt.Lt.Reddish and crew took off in 'Oscar' at 1155 hours for Skid Bombing, SARBE, Photography, SAR Search and a simulated Lindholme Gear drop. The flight lasted 5.20 hours Day and 2.05 hours Night.

27. & 28.01.65: 11.35 hours undetailed. After the 28th she didn't fly for a month because she was in for a minor service at 3271 airframe hours.

Sometime during March 201 Squadron moved from St.Mawgan to Kinloss. In May of that year after the move was complete WR977 joined the Kinloss Wing and she became a 'Pool' aircraft although still 'owned' by 201. This information is courtesy of Gerry Sage and Tony King who met up with her again briefly during this period.

WR977 as Oscar with 201 Squadron. Whilst a date has not been established for this picture, her poor condition and paint patches on her nose suggest that it was later in her tour with the unit. In Phase 2 configuration, the Union Jack on the nose signifies an overseas detachment. Possibly taken at RAF Kinloss. (Museum Collection)

04.03.65: Tom Haig records Oscar's airtest after the service, which was flown by the Officer Commanding 201 Squadron Wing Commander P.G.South. They also did some mandatory flying, the sortie length was 1 hour, from 1605 to 1705 hours.

14.03.65: 2.45 hour undetailed sortie.

16.03.65: Back with Tom Haig and Flt.Lt.Reddish's crew WR977 left the ground at 0845 for an L.R.O.F.E., Skid Bombing and a D.R.NAVEX lasting 15.15 hours, of which 5.20 hours were at night.

18.03.65: 12.19 hours flown, no details.

19.03.65: An 8.20 hour sortie with Flt.Lt.Reddish and crew for

WR977, Oscar in flight with a companion aircraft from 201 Squadron, believed to be over the Scottish coast. (Museum Collection)

With 42 Squadrpm. WR977 seen here taxying out at an air display, either at Woodford or Langar. (via Peter Howard)

Bombing and an Airways Exercise, they landed at Turnhouse and then returned to St.Mawgan, which was still perhaps their home at this time. Take off for this sortie was at 0924 hours.

23.03. - 10.04.65: Eight sorties recorded, totalling 81.15 flying hours.

14.04.65: Sqdn.Ldr.Haig took off in 'Oscar' at 0900 hours with his Captain Flt.Lt.Reddish for a 7.10 hour TORPEX. He notes 'TORPEX being a Torpedo Exercise where you drop a dummy torpedo and the launch picks it up and then you've done another chinograph square on the board.'

21. - 28.04.65: No details for 5 flights totalling 46.20 hours.

30.04.65: Tom Haig notes a 14.00 hour Exercise Red Knight sortie, 6 hours of which were at night. They left the ground at 1749 hours with John Reddish.

03. & 05.05.65: 28.40 hours flown, no details.

07.05.65: Sqdn.Ldr.Haig records a further 'Red Knight as Briefed' sortie lasting 8.45 hours day and 5.00 hours night. Chris Ashworth's book notes that this was a 'Submarine Barrier Exercise, and part of the ninth annual Fishplay series.' Take off for this sortie was at 2000 hours.

11. & 14.05.65: 26.20 hours flown, no details.

17.05.65: Sqdn.Ldr.Haig once again provides details for this sortie:
This was a sortie where we had the gulping engines, we did 14.30 hours day and 0.45 hour night.
The plan was to do a SAR to PLE, the Prudent Limitation of Endurance, which would have been about 16 hours plus, because the Shackleton could quite happily do over 18 hours on internal tanks. We had a faulty fuel guage, and the Flight Engineer said to the Skipper, 'We've got a faulty fuel guage and I'm not happy about the fuel in one tank'. So, the Skipper said perhaps we should go off task half an hour early, to which Pete Jackson (Flt. Eng.) replied 'How about another half hour for the wife and kids ?' So we went off task effectively an hour early. On our way over the Cairngorms one of the engines started to gulp, so we had to close it down

and land on three engines. As we taxied in another started to gulp, so we shut that down and taxied in on two engines. '977 sat on the pan looking sorry with oil dripping everywhere, and the airframe fitters later said that had we been airborne about another ten minutes or so, we would have lost a third. So, she nearly became a wreck that day ! The take off time for this sortie was 0335 hours.

15. - 28.05.65: Three sorties flown, for 12.25 hours, no further details.

09.06.65: WR977 left the ground at 1000 hours according to Sqdn.Ldr.Haig's log book for a 2.45 hour transit from Kinloss to St.Mawgan. Flt.Lt.Dave Perry was the pilot. That crew returned to Kinloss in WR990, but '977 must have returned with another crew.

10.06.65: 15.00 hours flown, no details.

13.06.65: Take off at 1127 hours. Details thanks to Sqdn.Ldr.Haig
> A SAR. with Dave Perry, he was the guy who was killed in the Moray Firth later that year, just before Christmas in XF704.
> We got airborne, and I was guest on the crew and was standing in for someone else, 'Trotter' Baxter, he had no sooner said to me 'Are you standing in ?' and I said 'I take your slot as of now.' he got in his car, drove off, the phone rang, and it was a call out to a trawler down off Spurn Point. A sick crewman, and we were just to supervise the helicopter flying in and out. But, as we got airborne I said to the crew 'Where's your cups ?' We were airborne without a single paper cup, or any sort of cup on the aircraft. So I mixed up the orange squash in the teapot and we passed that round and everybody had a drink out of the spout, and I took those dinky little light covers off the roof, washed them out, and served the tea up in those. As you see that was only 4.45 hours but we deliberately over rationed so that we'd have to get a new set, because even after we landed we were still on SAR for 24 hours, so we ate all the rations !

14.06.65: 6.00 hours flown, no details.

15.06.65: Sqdn.Ldr.Haig flew with Flt.Lt.Smith in 'Oscar' for Exercise 'Bright Eyes', they landed at Aalborg in Denmark and then returned to Kinloss. They took off at 1047 hours and the flight lasted 11.00 hours.

The following details for two flights are thanks to AEO Gerry Sage who flew in '977 when she was being shared by 120 Squadron as part of the Kinloss Wing. These are the only two flights we have recorded with that

Unit.

25.06.65: Take off 0638 hours, Sqdn.Ldr.Tony King was the pilot. 15.10 hours flying, Kinloss - Ops - Bodo.

26.06.65: 14.10 hours, no details but this was flown from Bodo, Norway.

27.06.65: Take off at 1500 hours, Sqdn.Ldr.King. 13.35 flying hours. Bodo - Ops - Bodo. Gerry Sage notes 'This was my last flight in a Shackleton'. In only two flights he'd completed 28.45 hours.

30.06.65: Sqdn.Ldr.Haig again flew with Flt.Lt.Smith, taking off at 0858 hours.

Sqdn.Ldr.Haig:

SURVEX land Bodo, 14.50 hours. We took off at 9 o'clock in the morning, we did 14.50 hours, landed at Bodo. We got airborne at 10 o'clock at night the next day and flew all night with our groundcrew on board as usual, landed at Bodo, the intention was to land back at Kinloss but we discovered that we hadn't got enough fuel. The groundcrew re+fuelled the aircraft and then we took straight off again. We did 30 hours flying in two days, I don't think it would be allowed today. That was my last flight in the aircraft, she must have gone off for Phase 3's at about that time.

Indeed this was WR977's last operational flight before Phase 3's, on July 2nd she transitted back to Kinloss at 0955 hours. She was officially handed over to A.V.Roe at Langar on the 13th at 3669.15 airframe hours.

Tom Haig had flown a total of 400.30 hours in '977.

9

PHASE 3'S

After leaving 201 Sqn. on 13th July 1965 WR977 returned to Langar to receive the final and most radical modifications to be carried out on the Mk.3 Shackleton, which would take until the following May.

The Phase 3 programme involved an almost complete re-build of major sections of the airframe. WR977, as with all British Mk.3's, was to have the following improvements: red anti-collision lights (roof mounted just forward of ECM mast and one under rear fuselage aft of tail skid); improved ECM; Honeywell Radar Altimeter (forward of anti-collision lights under rear fuselage, which actually entailed the removal of the tail skid); new UHF radio: SARBE (Search and Rescue Beacon - an improved version of SARAH); improved radio compass; gyro-compass GM Mk.7. However the major modifications changed much of the Shackleton's structure altogether. A further tactical Sonics station just forward of the trailing edge spar meant that the wardroom bulkhead was moved back to the flap-jack spar and in between the two spars the ASV operator was located. The wardroom was reduced in size by almost one third leaving a smaller galley, just one tier of three bunks and a rearward facing 'dinette' and led to the deletion of a small window on the port side where the ASV station now was.

The Shackleton's offesnsive capability was also increased with the introduction of the Mk.10 'Lulu' Nuclear Depth Bomb in addition to accoustic homing torpedoes. The heavy electrical loads meant the installation of a 'crate' of seven inverters had to be fitted in the starboard side of the nose. All these improvements meant the all-up weight of the already over-loaded aircraft was dramatically increased and reduced the 'stretched' take-off safety margin to practically nothing. The decision was made to give the Phase 3 assisted take off power and the unit chosen was the Bristol-Siddeley Viper 203 turbojet. After tests they were found to run successfully for limited periods on the same AVGAS fuel as the Rolls-Royce Griffons rather than the AVTUR normal for jets. The sturdy engine could withstand the lead deposits on the turbine blades and lower lubrication which the AVGAS provided.

The extra weight meant that the main spars had to be strengthened and subsequently involved re-skinning of large sections of the wings. The wiring for the rocket hardpoints under each wing being removed during this operation.

After a minor service at 3671.20 hrs. WR977 had four new engines fitted and a complete new set of propellors. Viper 203's serialled VL 203020/A66826 (Stbd.) and VL 203009/A668815 (Port) were installed and certificated on 2nd May 1966. Just prior to that on 29th April she was allocated to 42 Sqn. St. Mawgan under authority MC/A/299 at 3674.05 hrs. but wasn't actually picked up until May 3rd. She would have been painted in the 1966 colour scheme but with the introduction of Central Servicing and Aircraft Pooling no Sqdn. Number would have been painted on the aircraft, the only squadron identification being a small Sqdn. crest on a screw-on plate on each side of the aircraft's nose. Again '977 was the oldest of her type on the Unit.

Sqdn.Ldr.Julian Denham notes on the Phase 3:

The wing was very flexible, the tip tank moving up and down I suppose 6 feet with motion, which you got used to - though many of the crew could get very sick - usually not the pilots, as seeing out is a great help. We were subject to much abuse, both by the Navy and the RAF, denied air-conditioned quarters when serving overseas which was accorded to the Vulcan boys, on the basis that the aircraft wasn't airconditioned. It did have petrol driven heaters, when they worked, and filled the fuselage with petrol stink. The Navy called us crabs - we called them fishheads. The aircraft, sometimes called a f...ing Shacklef...ing bomber, was called also a 'hundred thousand rivets 'flying in formation'. Formation flying was hard physical work - I once flew in a vic of three around the island of Jamaica, much harder than a jet, because the control systems were manual, though the Mk.III had torque ailerons which the Mk.4 and Mk.2 did not have.

Despite the abuse, the aircraft was a potent weapon - how many of the public know that it was equipped to carry nuclear depth-charges? In the late 50s, there was a plan for it to be equipped to carry Skybolt nuclear missiles, as a back-up to the V-bombers, though perhaps fortunately this never happened. The large bomb-bay could carry a large variety of weaponry - nuclear and conventional depth charges, homing torpedoes, 1,000 lb bombs, markers, sonic detection buoys, and Lindholme rescue dinghies, and sono buoys.

There were many roles, and the crews had to be ready to carry out any at more or less any moment - no other aircraft in the RAF at the time could match this list: Maritime surveillance; Distant support; Close support, (of convoys); Offesnsive Operations - (attacking surface ships, and seeking and destroying submarines); Troop transport (where did they sit?!); ship and ground photography; Search & Rescue. Ground bombing - much more effective in the Aden protectorate of the 50s and 60s then the Hunter Squadron - one Shackleton on duty for 12 hours could deny the arab dissidents sleep, water, and farming, just by dropping one 1,000 lb bomb each hour near their village.

I recall weights of 105,000 lbs and then 113,000 lbs AUW take-off weight. The crews grew as well, from 10 to 12 and finally to 16 I remember. The poor old Griffons couldn't take it (Griffon - the most advanced in-line piston engine ever, vastly complex, and always likely to fail; coming back to base on three was entirely normal). Nowadays pilots are likely to complete their careers without ever having an engine failure - they are lucky!

Finally the decision was made to fit the two Viper engines in the outer nacelles initially to cope with the take-off. The engineer had control of the jet throttle, the pilots calling 'start the Vipers', 'Vipers 100%', 'Vipers 93%', 'Stop the Viper'. The Viper was exactly the same as the one in the Jet Provost, cheap and rugged; it ran on petrol from the normal tanks, instead of the paraffin of normal jets. 93% was 'Design rpm', the rpm when all the baldes are at their optimum angle of attack to the airflow within the engine, and the engine therefore at its most efficient. We ran the Vipers at idle rpm at all times in the circuit, and for attacks, and at high weights, (to provide quick back-up power).

Sq.Ldr.Denham has compiled a 'typical sortie' in a Shackleton Mk.3 Phase 3:

For an operational take-off, crews reported for briefing about 2 hours before. Engines were started about 20 minutes, before or even 40 minutes sometimes. Not just for the engines' benefit (a jet can take-off at once of course after engine start), but not pistons; the metal has to heat, the oil become liquid, the magnetos to be checked, but also of course all the electronics gear has also to be exercised and checked. Finally at take-off time (a lot of determination was required to get even this far by the captain, as so many factors ran against you) 2,750 rpm from the props., 'S' gear selected - with an almighty crash, Vipers 100% , Watermeth on (those tanks in the undercarriage bay behind the fire walls) maximum boost - 32 inches of mercury if my memory serves me, tremendous vibration throughout the airframe (so great that a friend of mine Harry Fisher, at Langar, at this point had the boltheads inside the undercarriage selector boxes break off, causing an electrical short, and the gear, undercarriage I should say retract on him!

Brakes Off and off you went. The Shackleton had what is called Performance 'X', i.e. totally unacceptable to civilian flying, as a situation developed as you went down the runway where, if an engine blew up, there was insufficient runway left to stop on, and the remaining engines had insufficient power to get you airborne. Well, if you were lucky, you got into the air, held your breath for the several minutes it took to climb to 1,000 feet, reduced the power, and began to settle into the flight. 18 hours and 50 minutes was my best, and there wasn't much fuel left at that point. Coffee arrived when the wheels went up, and a meal shortly after. The crew drew their own 'rations' the day before, and wonderful cooking transpired. Drinks every hour, with sandwiches, major snacks every 2 hours, and a main meal every 4 hours. We were much better off than the present Nimrod crews, with their heat-it-yourself

TV dinners. Circuit flying, called mandatory, was a 5 hour flight, as were bombing exercises, and some navigation exercises, and there were 10 hour flights, and 12 and 15 hours.

In theory, meals were taken in the Ward Room, and you tried to take a sleep on a bunk, leaving your colleague at the controls. I never had a lot of success with sleeping myself; as soon as my eyes closed, I felt the engines stop, and I was awake again! And of course on many flights you were too busy anyway.

Crossing the coast, the Captain called 'crossing the coast outbound checks' and the aircraft was made ready for operations. The gunner fired a few rounds, weapons were armed, flare chutes loaded, and many other checks. Even if you had a few hours to your patrol area, you were ready for action. At the other end of the flight, the call was 'Crossing the coast inbound checks' to make the aircraft safe to fly over land - i.e. not drop anything by mistake.

On patrol - lookout stations manned and briefed; detection policy determined - many different methods, worth a book in itself. It is night say, the radar has been turned off, now it is switched on. The radar operator peers at his orange screen; waves, or seagulls? No it is something more substantial perhaps the snorkel of a patrolling submarine. He applies his cursor, and calls 'contact bearing 230 degrees range 22 miles'. The crew is alive, the Captain calls 'Action Stations Action Stations Turning on'. All the crew automatically acknowledge, the co-pilot calling '2600' as he brings the rpm up to attack setting. The radar operator marks the position of the contact with chinagraph - 'Radar Standby!' so as not to alert the submarine. The turret is occupied, the navigators arm the likely weapons, the beam men standby the flares.

The aircraft completes its turn to face the target 'Running UP!' 'Radar ON' 'target 220 degrees 10 miles' 'Left 10' the aircraft is descending to 250 feet above the waves - it is pitch dark, and nothing can be seen from the cockpit. 5 miles 'Depthcharge attack' the navigator acknowledges, runs forward between the pilots to take position as bomb aimer. Radar continues to give the target position. 'Bomb Doors OPEN!' The aircraft sways as the doors open a trifle asymmetrically, then settles. The engineer has lit the Vipers. One mile - 'Flares Flares' off go the flares from the beam. Pyrotechnics smells fill the fuselage. The greenish flare light shows up the heaving waves, but the pilots are firmly flying on the instruments. 'Target sighted - snort - Left Left - Steady Steady - Right - Steady Steady Steady' (the bomb-aimer is watching the snorkel against a pattern of light lines on the sight glass; when lines no longer move against the target, he presses the tit - 'Bombs Gone' 'Camera running' calls the tactical navigator back at the nav station. The tail lookout 'Fifty Fifty no line!' a stick of depth charges has straddled the target, the aircraft buckets as the shock wave hits it. 'Flares off' 'Bomb Doors closed!' '18 inches' (i.e. power to climb away) 'Follow up attack' Climb to 500 feet - minumum speed 160 knots - 'Turning On' apply 60° of bank eyes glued to the artificial horizon and ASI - 'Running Up', and here we go again.

Mind you, I have known it when all this goes gloriously wrong - not many of these OK calls got made, and the instructor (frequently me) calls plaintifly 'Somebody say something, even if it's only Happy Christmas!.

10

PHASE 3 AND 42 SQUADRON

01.05.66: 2.45 hour undetailed flight, but this was probably an airtest after the port and starboard undercarriages had been changed on this date.

03.05.66: Flt.Lt.Fred Weaver again met up with '977 when he and Flt.Lt.Jack Greenwood and crew, including Sgt.Phil Marston (now Sqdn.Ldr.) went to collect her from Langar. She left Langar as a six engined Phase 3 Shackleton at 1635 hours for the 1.25 hour transit back to St.Mawgan.

03.05. - 23.06.66: No flying due to a Major service being necessary. This was due at 3526 airframe hours but was not carried out until 3675.30 hours.

23. & 24. 06.66: Two undetailed flights totalling 2.05 hours. After this for reasons unknown she didn't fly for a month.

20.07.66: Flt.Lt.Weaver and Flt.Lt.Eggleton flew a 1.15 hour airtest possibly after work having been carried out on the major Service. 40 minutes of the flight was instrument flying, making a three engine landing with an asymmetric NDB and ILS approaches.

21.07.66: WR977 left the ground at 0945 hours with Flt.Lt.Weaver and Crew 5, details also provided by Phil Marston who was an AEO on this crew, for an 'Airways Exercise' flying to Kinloss, on to Leuchars in Scotland and then back to St.Mawgan. Flt.Lt.Weaver records the return legs as the next day, the 22nd. Total flying time was 5.55 hours, with a QGH and a GCA approach.

25.07.66: Flt.Lt.Weaver flew with Phil Marston and Crew 5, taking off at 1835 hours for a Day/Night Mandatory. They flew 2.25 hours Day and 1.45 hours Night. They made a flapless Day landing, and a four and three engine Night landing, and 30 minutes Simulated Instrument/Cloud flying. However a further flight must have been made, bringing the daily total to

7.45 hours.

26.07.66: Flt.Lt.Weaver and Eggleton flew a 6.45 hour flight for O.T. and a Stage II Exercise, flying to Bovingdon and then returning to St.Mawgan, with Crew 3. Thirty minutes was 'Actual' Instrument/Cloud flying.

27.07.66: Back with Phil Marston and Crew 5, Flt.Lt.Weaver lifted WR977 off from a St.Mawgan runway at 1100 hours for OT, a Stage II Exercise and SAR Searches, and Day Bombing. Flight duration 5.30 hours.

29.07.66: Flt.Lt.Weaver and Eggleton and Crew 3, with the AOC of 19 Group onboard for OT and Ship Photography but the flight only lasted 1.55 hours because they had to RTB due to 'Loss of Electrics.'

03.08.66: Phil Marston flew with Flt.Lt.Eggleton for a Mk.1C Sonics Evaluation lasting 8.50 hours taking to the air at 0900 hours.

04. - 25.08.66: Five undetailed flights for 20.10 hours.

27.08.66: Flt.Lt.Weaver logs a flight with Flt.Lt.Jarvis and a 'Basic Crew 5' for Ship Photography of Sir Francis Chichester and three Navy Day Displays, two at Plymouth and one at Portsmouth. The flight lasted 6.45 hours.

29.08. - 13.09.66: Three undetailed flights for a total of 17.30 hours.

14.09.66: Flt.Lt.Weaver and Crew 5 flew with Flt.Lt.Elias for a Crew Classification lasting 4.30 hours, with 2.15 hours at the controls for each pilot. Total time for this day was 8.40 hours meaning a further flight must have taken place. This period was one of the most intensive of WR977's career, several flights a day being a regular occurrance.

16. - 25.09.66: 18.40 hours flown in four flights.

WR977 at Butterworth, Malaysia, believed to be on the way to Majunga.

27.09.66: Flt.Lt.Weaver and Phil Marston's Crew 5, with Air Commodore Wheelan, took '977 for a CASEX B1 and Gunnery (indicating that the Hispano cannon were fitted), Night Bombing, OT, Air Plans and Ship Photography. The flight lasted 7.40 hours Day and 2.20 hours Night. They made a four and three engined Night Landing.

29.09.66: The same crew as the previous flight, minus the Air Commodore, flew a CASEX C1 & B5 Bombing sortie, for 7.50 hours with 4.00 hours 'Actual' Instrument Flying.

29.09. - 03.10.66: 17.35 hours flown, no details,

04.10.66: Sqdn.Ldr.Phil Marston records a Search and Rescue for 'PUFFIN', a fishing boat, with Sqdn.Ldr.Roberts, the flight lasted 6.50 hours. However no other details of the operation are available other than that they landed at Lann Bihoue, near Brest, Brittany, France.

05.10.66: A CASEX A35 flown from Lann Bihoue, landing there after 8.00 hours flying.

06.10.66: WR977 returned to St.Mawgan, completing a Stage II Mandatory Exercise, landing back in Cornwall after 5.00 hours.

11. - 14.10.66: Three flights totalling 28.20 hours but no further details.

18.10.66: Phil Marston records 12.05 hours on Exercise 'Snapdragon' although further details for this exercise are not available. After this sortie she had a No.2 front prop. changed at 3868.15 airframe hours, and didn't fly again until the 21st.

21.10.66: This is a significant date in the life of WR977 as it was the first recorded time that she met Flt.Sgt.'Jock' Hosie, a Flight Engineer. He and his family were to have a considerable effect on the eventual restoration of the aircraft 25 years on from this date. George Hosie remained in regular contact with '977 many years after he had finished flying her.

This was also the first flight in the aircraft for a friend of 'Jock's', Co-Pilot Dave Lawrence. He notes

> I think Jock and I more or less considered WR977 our aeroplane. While we were on 42 Squadron, particularly in the early part of our tour we seemed to fly it quite often, but it was also the one we took on our first long detachment to Singapore and then Majunga.

This flight was a Conversion and Mandatory Training sortie for Dave Lawrence and Jock Hosie to convert onto the Mk.3 Phase 3. it lasted 1.50 hours Day, and the Captain was a Flt.Lt.Patterson. A further flight must have taken place bringing the daily total to 3.30 hours.

25.10.66: Flt.Sgt.Hosie and Dave Lawrence again record a Conversion and Mandatory Training flight, this time with Flt.Lt.Bethel, lasting 2.15 hours. Again a further flight must have taken place bringing the daily total to 10.40 hours.

27.10.66: 4.15 hours but no further details. After this she didn't fly for a month, there is no explaination.

30.11.66: Flt.Sgt.Hosie records a flight of 3.40 hours with Flt.Lt.Patterson, again for more Conversion and Mandatory Training.

07.12.66: 3.30 hour flown, no details.

08.12.66: Flt.Lt.Weaver flew with Flt.Lt.Jarvis and Crew 5 (minus Phil Marston) for a 2.35 hour Day Mandatory flight. They made a four and three engine Day landing and QGH and ILS approach, plus one asymmetric ILS. Daily total hours 5.10 hours.

After this flight she is noted as having a Primary Service and new No.1 engine fitted at 3899 airframe hours.

19.12.66: Jock Hosie records a 1.15 hour Airtest after the service with another pilot from WR977's past, now Officer Commanding 42 Squadron, Wing Commander Parry-Davies. She also flew with Flt.Lt.Weaver on this date, and Phil Marston with Crew 5, flying Air Vice Marshal Barraclough AOC 19 Group and Major General Grant plus five passengers to Gibraltar, a flight time of 6.35 hours and making a GCA. Fred Weaver recalls:

> This was a VIP flight. I flew Air Vice Marshal Barraclough, Major General Grant and six other passengers to Gibraltar. The only thing about this, being a night take off in thick fog. Taxying very slowly to the threshold of runway 310 and aligning the aircrfat on the centre green lights for a blind take off. At St.Mawgan a road crosses the main runway about half way along. It is guarded by traffic lights. During the one or two times that I took off in these conditions whilst I was at St.Mawgan, the thought that some driver might ignore them worried me a little. However on this occasion we were soon airborne and at a height of about 300 to 400 feet we broke out into a clear starlit night . An uneventful flight to Gibraltar followed.

20.12.66: The same crew brought the Air Vice Marshal and the Major General back to the UK, but this time with six other passengers. The flight lasted 6.05 hours, They made a QGH and GCA on return.

21.12.66: 5.05 hours flown, no details but after which she had a short break over the Christmas period.

11

'BRAVELY IN ACTION' - WR977 ON ACTIVE SERVICE

WR977's only participation in an active war situation occurred at the beginning of 1967. She went, with three other MR.3 aircraft to Madagascar (Malagasy) to relieve the MR.2's deployed there for the "Beira Patrols", officially named "Operation MIZAR". Explaination of the situation and operations is first given by Jack Greenwood who flew several Mizar Ops. in WR977:

> After the Unilateral Declaration of Independence (UDI) by the government of Ian Smith. An attempt was made to bring them to heel by cutting off their oil supplies. Since Rhodesia had no coastline it was decided to blockade the port of Beira through which their oil was supplied. The Royal Navy supplied the ships for the blockade and the task of the Royal Air Force was to intercept and identify all tankers which might have been attempting to break the blockade. Their details were then passed to the Navy.

In his book Chris Ashworth notes that by the time WR977 was participating, the Navy Task Force was led by HMS Eagle. 'Each sortie was planned to cover 130,000 square miles of ocean on the approaches to Beira by flying a 'Creeping Line Ahead' using an 80nm track spacing.'

The four aircraft and their crews were based at Majunga airfield in Madagascar. Gil Harman who was flown out in early March by Transport Command and subsequently flew several Mizar Ops. in WR977 recalls:

> At this time the groundcrew at Majunga lived at the 'Village Touristique' in holiday cabins on the beach and had their meals in the restaurant at the 'hotel' - if you can call it that. The take offs for Mizars were fairly early in the morning before it got too hot - take off was a bit dicey at full load in the heat of the day. The surveillance sorties in the Beira Channel were about 12 hours and on returning to Majunga we 'buzzed' the Village Touritique so that the groundcrew could nip out to the airfield to meet us. I buzzed a bit lower than most until the authorities complained and then we behaved more circumspectly.
>
> At that time the SNCO's lived in the 'Maison de Maire' - the Mayor's House and the officers were in another French maison - where the plumbing was grotty, to say the least.
>
> On the Mizars at the end of the patrol, we sometimes carried out a mail drop to the frigate on station with mail packed in small Lindholme containers joined by a floating cord.

Jack Greenwood also notes that

> During the Beira patrols it was sometimes difficult to pass position reports, particularly in the early morning, but when no one else would answer, Rhodesian air traffic control would come up loud and clear from Salisbury and offer to relay our position back to Majunga (which we gratefully accepted) !!" and "In our Officers Mess, the Villa Desiree, my AEO, Flt.Lt.Bill Hoare delighted in answering the phone with 'Hoare of the House of Desire.'

WR977 was to complete four months in the heat of Majunga, after which the burden again fell on the MR.2's. Dave Lawrence comments on the Beira Patrols "Whether much was achieved is for the politicians to decide!'

02.01.67: Sqdn.Ldr.Roberts was the pilot with Dave Lawrence in the right-hand seat, and Jock Hosie was the Engineer for the first stage to Gibraltar, 4 hours Day, 2.30 hours Night.

Later that day they departed Gibraltar for Akrotiri in Cyprus but had to return to Gib. with an oil leak having only 1.10 hours flying. Flt.Sgt.Hosie's personal notes reveal the problem:

> WR977, TRANSIT ST.MAWGAN TO SINGAPORE 2-7 JAN.'67. No.1 ENGINE - INTERSHAFT SEAL LEAKING - CHANGED AT GIB., AGAIN AT KHORMAKSAR - ON LAST LEG TO KHORMAKSAR BLACK OIL HAD SPREAD TO OUTER COWLING TOP AND SIDES AND EXTENDED OVER TOP OF MAINPLANE LEADING EDGE - A FEW DRIPS - NOT ON TAILPLANE. OIL CONSUMPTION PROVED SAME AS OTHER ENGINES.

03.01.67: '977 and her crew finally left Gib. and she behaved on the flight to Akrotiri arriving there 10 hours later.

04.01.67: The next stage was Akrotiri - Khormaksar still apparently behaving. The flight lasted 8.25 hours, all Day flying, and at sometime during those hours Jock Hosie made notes from which we know that

> WR977's All Up Weight (AUW) for the transit was 103,000 lbs. and she was flying at Flight Level 20. They climbed to F.L.80, which took 13 minutes and used 140 gallons of fuel.

05.01.67: Khormaksar to Gan leg. The flying time was 11.35 hours including 3 hours Night flying. Here Ron Cole a Ground technician notes that he stayed with XF711 'C' and crew to relieve 205 Squadron permanently deployed there flying MR.2s in order for them to have their

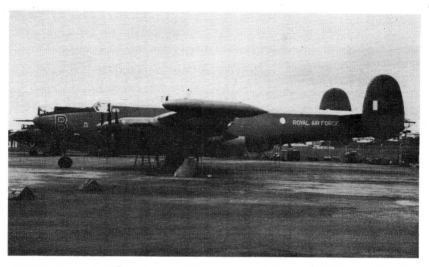

WR977, Bravo with 42 Squadron, not 203 as often noted. Note pre-1968 Bitteswell mods. and unit badge on the nose. With guns fitted and her surroundings suggest the picture was taken in Majunga or perhaps Luga.

Villa Desiree, the Officers Mess in Majunga. (Jack Greenwood)

73

The Air Traffic Control Tower at Majunga Airport. (Jack Greenwood)

An overview of the dispersal area at Majunga. (Jack Greenwood)

74

50th Anniversary Celebrations. They were to be on SAR standby.

06.01.67: WR977 went on to Changi with her crew. Flight time was 8 hours Day and 2 hours Night.

12.01.67: 4.40 hours, no details.

Jock Hosie was flying in XF707 and XF711 with Flt.Lt.Birch and his crew on these dates for familiarisation, O.T. and gunnery. So it would seem that Hispano cannon were fitted to the aircraft, so perhaps WR977 was employed on similar duties. She remained at Changi. Dave Lawrence notes:"Very little flying was done in Singapore, and due to a pilot being sick, I did not fly WR977 to Majunga". This would seem to explain the crew change.

24.01.67: 4.15 hours, no details.

29.01.67: Jock Hosie now remained with Flt.Lt.Birch as pilot, the Crew Captain being Flt.Lt.Wilson, and returned to '977 for a flight of 1.45 hours from Changi to Butterworth. From there she flew to Gan, an 8.45 hour flight. The daily total was therefore 10.30 hours.

30.01.67: With the same crew she made a 9.45 hour flight on the last stage to her destination and new home for four months, Majunga.

02.02.67: Jock Hosie records '977's first 'Mizar' Operation, logged as 'MIZAR AND SHIP CO-OP'. The sortie was flown by Flt.Lt. Birch and lasted 11.15 hours.

06.02.67: This was the same crew for another Mizar Op. but she had to RTB after 6.20 hours (One hour of which was at night), this was due to a hydraulic leak.

25.02.67: She hadn't flown since the 6th, obviously due to repairs after the RTB This sortie is undetailed but lasted 11.45 hours and was obviously a further Mizar Op.

28.02.67: 11.10 hours, no details but again a Mizar Op.

03.03.67: Flt.Lt.Birch and Flt.Sgt.Hosie's crew completed an 11.50 hour Mizar and Ship Co-Op.

Although flying times for undetailed sorties would not normally be listed, in this case it is felt important to show sortie lengths and intensity of those flights. This was the only time WR977 was involved in a conflict.

11.03.67: 12.00 hours.

14.03.67: 12.15 hours.

19.03.67: 12.45 hours.

22.03.67: 11.55 hours. After this sortie No.3 engine was replaced at 4083.20 hours, she didn't fly again for nearly a week.

27.03.67: Flt.Lt.Greenwood flew '977 again, Flt.Lt.Dave Henken was his Co-Pilot (later famed for commanding the last operational Squadron of Shackletons employed in the 1970's and 80's on Airborne Early Warning). This sortie was an 11.35 hour Mizar Op. Jack Greenwood notes that Flt.Lt.Henken was 'much in demand when we were not flying because, unlike the officially appointed so-called interpreter he could speak fluent French !'

01.04.67: Flt.Lt.Jack Greenwood again flew a Mizar Op., this time of 11.25 hours, including 2 hours Night Flying.

06.04.67: 12.15 hours.

09.04.67: 11.30 hours flown on Mizar by Flt.Lt.Gil Harman.

13.04.67: 1.00 hour flight whose length may suggest problems, because after this flight No.1 front prop. was replaced at 4131.05 airframe hours.

17.04.67: 12.20 hours. this was WR977's last Mizar Op. flown by Flt.Lt.Gil Harman before the end of the detachment. Dave Lawrence notes that a route change for the return trip was necessary:

> This route was eventually chosen, after various others were considered, because the Arab - Israeli War prevented us flying the more normal route via Aden and over Egypt etc.

22.04.67: Flt.Sgt. Hosie again joined WR977 for the return legs, Flt.Lt.Keith Jarvis was the pilot, Dave Lawrence was Co-Pilot, Tony Davies was an AEOp, and the Crew Captain was Flt.Lt.Wilson. this sortie was a 6.30 hour transit from Majunga to Entebbe in Uganda.

23.04.67: The same crew flew her on to Kano in Nigeria, a flight time of 7.55 hours.

Gil Harman flies WR977 low over Majunga beach in April 1967. Gil Harman notes that they flew low over the beach to alert the groundcrew, who were accommodated in the beach huts on their arrival. (via Dave Lawrence)

77

24.04.67: This was a transit to the USAF base at Wheelus in Libya. However on arrival WR977 misbehaved again with nosewheel problems. Tony Davies note that they had 'problems with the customs at Kano, and then a reluctance for the nosewheel to indicate locked down on the approach to USAF Wheelus in Tripoli.'

The indication for undercarriage locked down is three green lights in the cockpit, one for each U/C leg. They show red when the undercarriage is between locks.

Dave Lawrence recalls:

> An incident enroute occurred at Wheelus Air Force Base (a USAF base in those days). On arrival there, we obtained a red light for the nosewheel, indicating that it wasn't locked down properly. Nothing we did could obtain the green light, although the gear appeared to be down. The 'emergency' was declared to ATC at Wheelus, who then ordered us to hold off for a while. The reason for this was to recall all their airborne fighter aircraft, mainly Phantoms, a large number of which were operating at the local range. These all have to be recovered before we could land, in case we blocked the runway with a collapsed nosewheel. We must have been the cause of the wastage of a lot of fuel, weapons and sorties for the fighters! Eventually we were able to land, the landing being quite normal. However, there WAS a structural failure in the down locking mechanism which needed proper repair, which couldn't be done at Wheelus, (not quickly, anyway). Special permission was granted by HQ for us to fly to Luqa, Malta the next day, with the undercarriage locked down. This was completed without incident, and repairs were effected overnight by 203 Squadron personnel.

25.04.67: Wheelus to Luqa transit with the ground locks in with her crew. The transit lasted 1.30 hours Day.

26.04.67: The final stage of the journey home, 7.00 hours from Luqa to St.Mawgan.

WR977 at RAF St.Mawgan in April 1967, shortly after the Majunga detachment.
(via R. B. Ashworth)

WR977 of 42 Squadron and WB845 of MOTU prepare for their joint sortie to look for Gypsy Moth IV, at RAF St. Mawgan, May 25th 1967. (via Dave Lawrence)

12

WR977 BACK IN BLIGHTY

On her arrival home in the UK WR977 was due for a minor service, but was given a 70 hour flying hour extension. No.4 engine was changed at 4173.17 hours.

09.05.67: 12.20 hours flown, no details available.

14.05.67: WR977 now returned to Flt.Lt.Weaver and Crew 5 with Phil Marston, but with Flg.Off.Kemble as Co-Pilot. This sortie was an Oil Recce Flight on Operation 'MOP-UP' after the Torrey Canyon ran aground and broke up, Chris Ashworth's book notes:

> The supertanker Torrey Canyon, carrying 118,000 tons of crude oil, went aground on the Seven Stones Reef off Land's End. The ship subsequently broke in two, spreading oil over the sea and on to the Cornish beaches. Operation Mop-Up was started as soon as the seriousness of the situation was appreciated. Shackletons of No.42 Squadron (helped by No.206 for the first week), with MOTU providing a back-up, flying daily 'dawn' reconnaissance to check the extent and movement of the oil slicks. The completed charts were then packed into a container, which was dropped in Plymouth Sound for onward transmission to the Control Centre.

It was also a SAR Search for the yacht 'CARYS'. They flew 8.55 hours, making an NDB and ILS on return.

16. & 22.05.67: 19.40 hours flown. No details. After the sortie on the 22nd she had reached 4214 airframe hours. She had No.2 Engine and No.3 Front prop. changed.

23.05.67: 45 minutes flown, no details but more than likely an airtest after the component change.

Bravo Searches For Chichester - 24. & 25.05.67:

42 squadron were involved in the searches for Sir Francis Chichester in his yacht 'Gypsy Moth IV' when he disappeared at the end of his epic round the world voyage. WR977 took part in two searches.

24.05.67: Mr. R.L. Langrish having left the RAF, was a Warrant Officer in the ATC at this time, he managed to get a trip in WR977. He recalls:

It was an early morning take off, with the aircraft fully loaded with fuel. I remember reporting from the beam, the amount of overflow from the discharge pipes. A six engine take off saw us destined for the Bay of Biscay. It was a nice dry morning and the mission was to act as SAR standby for fighters on their way back to the UK from the Middle East. I remember that we had a rendezvous with a P2 7V Neptune of the Portugese Air Force and remained on station in that area until the fighters had gone by.

After we were taken off task, we began the transit home, when we were re-tasked by 19 Group at Mountbatten to look for Sir Francis Chichester.

I remember the further we travelled North and West, the worse the weather became. I remember passing over the stern section only, of a bulk carrier or tanker in primer paint, under tow in very heavy seas.

We climbed to seven thousand feet to avoid the thunder storms, I also remember that I was returning out of the nose when in one of the clouds there was a lot of buffeting on the aircraft, and in three evil steps the aircraft sank to three thousand feet, not a very pleasant experience!!

We reached an allocated area to start the search, which I remember was on the creeping line ahead system. This search carried on, many times going down to sea level, to check out radar contacts, which on many occasions was just driftwood, until it was calculated that fuel levels dictated that we return to base.

As I recall, the flight was just over 23 hours long.

Cover of Jock Hosies Log Book.

25.05.67: The information has been given by several of crew members from both aircraft, but initial indications and log book details for the search came from Engineer on the sortie, Jock Hosie.

Dave Lawrence notes:

> I was the Co-Pilot on that particular sortie, the Crew Captain being Flt.Lt.Eric Seales (Navigator Captain), and the First Pilot being Flt.Lt.Keith Jarvis. Almost certainly the Engineer would have been Jock Hosie who was Flight Engineer for our crew, (Jock was a good friend of mine).
>
> The sortie involved two aircraft, ourselves from 42 Squadron with WR977, and a crew from MOTU, with WB845, a T.4 (not a Mk.1 really).
>
> Both aircraft carried representatives of the press (we had people from the 'better' newspapers, like the Telegraph, etc., whilst the T.4 carried people from the 'other' papers, Daily Mirror, Sun etc.!!!)
>
> Anyway the two aircraft were allocated adjoining areas to search, and Gypsy Moth IV was actually found by the T.4.
>
> They called us over, and together we flew past the yacht a few times. As far as I remember we were under orders not to remain there too long, and annoy Chichester. Apparently it was thought that he wouldn't be too happy with too much attention.
>
> Our flight time for the sortie was 9.15 hours, I suppose the flight time of the T.4 was about the same.

Apparently the location occurred at around 0830 hours on the morning of the 25th. Peter Morris, a Navigator on the T.4 notes:

> I was the Navigator on WB845 piloted by Sqdn.Ldr.Archie Kinch. This was a T.4 of MOTU, the other Navigator with me was Dave White.
>
> We took off from St.Mawgan with a number of reporters on board. We located the Gypsy Moth IV about half way through the area we were searching. A previous arrangement had been made that whoever located Gypsy Moth IV first would home the other aircraft in before any reporters could take any photographs, this gave me a good opportunity to take some photos with my 8mm cine camera.

Returning to Dave Lawrence:

> The only photo I recall seeing from this sortie is the one enclosed. I cannot remember where I got it. However, the press faked the shot, - I remember quite clearly realising this as soon as I saw the picture. I remember we were never in this particular position with the T.4 to have such a photo taken, they obviously superimposed the aircraft on a picture of the yacht. You can also see that the horizon below the aircraft looks a bit odd. I think this photo did appear in the newspaper.

WR977 overflies Gypsy Moth IV, May 25th 1967. (Press Association via Dave Lawrence)

SECTION 3

Year		AIRCRAFT		Pilot	Aircrew Duty	Flight Details	Day (1)	Night (2)	Captain (3)	Spare (4)
Month	Date	Type & Mk.	No.							
					Totals brought forward		359:55	52:30		
APRIL	14	SHACKLETON 3.3	XF707	FLT LT JARVIS	ENGINEER	MANDATORY (MAJUNGA)			1:15	F.L.WILSON
APRIL	19	SHACKLETON 3.3	XF707	FLT LT JARVIS	ENGINEER	MIZAM	11:05		F.L.WILSON
APRIL	20	SHACKLETON 3.3	WR977	FLT LT JARVIS	ENGINEER	MAJUNGA – ENTEBBE	6:30		F.L.WILSON
APRIL	23	SHACKLETON 3.3	WR977	FLT LT JARVIS	ENGINEER	ENTEBBE – KANO	7:55		F.L.WILSON
APRIL	24	SHACKLETON 3.3	WR977	FLT LT JARVIS	ENGINEER	KANO – WHEELUS (UN-LOADED)	4:30	8:30	F.L.WILSON
APRIL	25	SHACKLETON 3.3	WR977	FLT LT JARVIS	ENGINEER	WHEELUS – LUQA (U/C-LOCKED DOWN)	1:30		F.L.WILSON
APRIL	26	SHACKLETON 3.3	WR977	FLT LT JARVIS	ENGINEER	LUQA – ST. MAWGAN	7:00		F.L.WILSON
				SUMMARY FOR APRIL 67	SHACKLETON MK.3		58:30	8:45		
				UNIT :- 42 SQDN						
				DATE:- 20 MAY 67						
				SGN:-						
AIR ENGINEER LDG 42 SQDN										
☆ FLIGHT COMMANDER 42 SQDN										
MAY	25	SHACKLETON 3.3	WR977	FLT LT JARVIS	ENGINEER	CHICHESTER	9:15			
				SUMMARY FOR MAY 67	SHACKLETON MK.3					
				UNIT :- 42 SQDN						
				DATE:- 14 JUNE 67						
				SGN:-						
AIR ENGINEER LDG 42 SQDN										
☆ FLIGHT COMMANDER 42 SQDN										
					Totals carried forward		397:40	56:15		

Jock Hosie's Log Book and the Chichester Search entry, as flown on WR977.
Note the Majunga return transits for WR977 earlier in the Log. (thanks to Shirley Hosie)

T.4 WB845 taken from WR977 during the Chichester search May 25th 1967.
(via Dave Lawrence)

Harry Hickling also flew in the MOTU T.4 and notes that the photograph of the T.4 which appeared in the Times, was taken by a photographer in WR977.

Many thanks to all those people who sought and found information about this sortie.

Back on Ops.

27.05.67: Phil Marston records a flight of 7.05 hours on Exercise 'SNAPDRAGON' with Flt.Lt.Weaver and Flt.Lt.Kemble. This was a surveillance sortie. Total flying time for the day is noted as 9.15 hours, suspiciously close to that of the previous day, although it may simply be a further flight of 2.10 hours.

30.05.67: Phil Marston records a 4.40 hour Mandatory sortie with Flt.Lt.Birch and Flt.Lt.Jarvis. By the end of this sortie the 70 hour extension prior to the minor service was up, so at 4238.25 airframe hours she was grounded for the service.

07.07.67: This is an undetailed flight but at only 1.00 hour duration, and as the first recorded after the service it was probably an airtest. She may have had a re-paint as subsequent photo's show her in a far better condition than after her stint in Madagascar.

18.07.67: Three flights are detailed for this date, but there is no indication of which order they occurred in.

Flt.Sgt.Hosie records a 4.05 hour flight for a Stage II exercise and day Bombing with Flt.Lt.Harris at the helm. Flt.Lt.Weaver, Kemble and Crew 5 (minus Phil Marston) for a 1.00 hour Day Mandatory sortie, making one 3 engine Day landing. The same crew (probably later the same day) carried out a Night Mandatory sortie, making a four and three engined Night landing, which lasted 1.40 hours. The daily total was 7.45 hours.

20.07.67: 8.00 hours undetailed.

24.07.67: 12.00 hours flown in total. Some are undetailed, but as illustrated on the 18th of the month, several flights with different crews could take place in one day. Flt.Sgt.Hosie recorded a 8.20 hours with Flt.Lt.Jarvis for O.T. and a CASEX.

26. & 28.07.67: 23.25 hours flown, no details.

01.08.67: Again two flights were made on this date, there is no indication of which way round they occurred.

Flt.Sgt.Hosie flew WR977 with Flt.Lt.Jarvis again for further O.T., Stage II and Day Bombing, flying time was 9.10 hours.

Flt.Lt.Weaver also records a 310 hour Day/Mandatory sortie, over 2 hours of which were flown at night, made with Flg.Off.Denten and Crew 5. They completed a 3 engined Day and 3 and 4 engine Night landings, also an Asymmetric QGH and GCA. Total time for the day was 12.20 hours, 13.15 hours were recorded.

03. & 04.08.67: A total of 12.55 hours flying.

08.08.67: Jock Hosie flew with Flt.Lt.Daniels and Dave Lawrence for CCCB Select Crew Classification, Tony Davies an AEOp on the crew notes: 'Crew 2 of 42 Squadron became, I believe the first SELECT CREW in 18 Group.' The flight lasted 6.00 hours. The total hours for the 8th were 12.55 hours.

10.08.67: Phil Marston records a 3.40 hour Day Bombing and Ship Photography with Flt.Lt.Kidson at the controls. Total flying time was 9.30 hours.

14. - 29.08.67: Five flights undetailed for a total of 26.35 hours.

01.09.67: Flt.Lt.Weaver flew WR977 with Crew 5 and Flg.Off.Kemble on O.T., Day Bombing, 'Skids', Stage II and Ship Photography, lasting 5.15 hours. They made a GCA on return and 5 hours of the sortie was instrument/cloud flying 'Actual'.

Ramp picture of WR977, Bravo, 42 Squadron September 1967. (via R.B. Ashworth)

06. - 14.09.67: Five flights, 35.20 hours, after which No.1 and 3 engines were changed at 4401 airframe hours, along with both Viper jets.

26.09. - 18.10.67: 37.30 hours flown in 7 sorties.

20.10.67: Phil Marston completed a sortie with Flt.Lt.Eggleton from Ballykelly to St.Mawgan, 15 minutes Day and 2.00 hours Night. A transit out to Northern Ireland must have been made at some time during the previous undetailed section.

24.10.67: Flt.Sgt.Hosie flew again with Flt.Lt.Jarvis for an 'OP-EVAL' (Operational Evaluation) flying 10.15 hours Day and 1.25 hours Night.

26.10.67: Jock Hosie flew WR977 again for a 1.20 hour Night Mandatory sortie with Flt.Lt.Patterson.

31.10. - 07.11.67: Five flights, making 30.40 hours undetailed. After the flight on the 7th No.2 engine was changed at 4484.28 airframe hours, and she didn't fly again until the 10th.

10.11.67: 50 minutes flying time, probably an airtest.

13. - 21.11.67: Four flights totalling 23.20 hours.

18.11.67: No flight but the port main undercarriage leg was changed at 4497.04 airframe hours, scheduled for replacement at 8497 airframe hours.

23.11.67: Flt.Lt.Weaver took off with Flg.Off.Kemble, Phil Marston and Crew 5, and with Group Captain Barratt onboard for Vertical Photography, WESTAXE, CASEX C1 and Day Mandatory flying. They made a three engine Day landing and an Asymmetric QGH and GCA, plus 1 hour of the flying time was 'Actual' instrument flying. Flight time, 4.15 hours.

24.11.67: Flt.Lt.Weaver again flew 'Bravo' with Flg.Off.Kemble and a 'Mixed Crew' for a Day Mandatory sortie, flying for 1.30 hours, half of which was flown on instruments. He made a further flight that day for a Night Mandatory of 1.35 hours, making a four and a three engine landing. More flights were also made with other Crews on this date as the daily flight total was 5.45 hours.

30.11. - 05.12.67: Three flights making 14.50 hours. After which at 4535.51 airframe hours No.2 front prop. was changed.

07. & 12.12.67: 8 hours flown, no details. After the 12th she did not fly again until the end of the month due to No.3 Rear, and No.4 Front and Rear props. being changed.

03.01.68: 9.30 hours flown, but no details. After this a new No.4 engine was fitted and she didn't fly again until the 17th.

17. - 19.01.68: 8.30 hours flown.

19. - 23.01.68: No.'s 1 and 2 Rear props. replaced.

23.01.68: 6.45 hours, no details.

25.01.68: Flt.Lt.Weaver took WR977 and Crew 5 for a 2.20 hour Night Mandatory. They made a three and four engine landing and an Asymmetric NDB and GCA. This was Phil Marston's last flight in WR977 he'd flown 131.25 hours in her since he went to collect her from Langar as a Phase 3 almost two years earlier.

13

WR977 ON CARIBEX '68

The details for this detachment are provided by Tony Davies who was AEOp on '977 for some of the sorties, Dave Lawrence who flew as her Co-Pilot for some of the time, Ron Cole a Ground Engineer on the detachment, and Fred Weaver who didn't fly '977 on the trip, but gives details of the detachment itself.

Early in 1968 a rumour had started that there was to be a 'CARIBEX' in February, to be based on the Island of Curacao in the Dutch Antilles, North of Venezuela. Bomb-bay fuel tanks were required for certain legs of the journey which meant the aircraft were operating at their maximum all-up weight of 108,000 lbs. Three aircraft were chosen for the detachment, WR977 was lead.

Fred Weaver notes:

> B - WR977 was flown by 42 Squadron Commanding Officer, Wg.Cdr.Ryan; E - XF730 was flown by Flt.Lt.Terry Earl; F - XF706 I flew, carrying a VIP passenger. The Air Officer Commanding No.19 group, Air Vice Marshal Lapsley.
>
> First we all went to London to be fitted out in very good quality uniforms (On loan I hasten to add). Not in RAF Blue but in a kind of brown colour, very similar to that of the Americans.

Technical back-up was provided by fifteen groundcrew.

07.02.68: WR977 and her two companion aircraft departed St.Mawgan flown by Wg.Cdr.Ryan for the first leg of her trip. This was a 7.15 hour transit to Lajes.

08.02.68: Bravo left Lajes behind, and arrived at Kindley Air Force Base in Bermuda 12.20 hour later. Ron Cole notes:

> They'd obviously seen the odd one go through before but to have three Mk.3's turn up within half an hour of each other must have raised a few eyebrows ! Some American engineer came up to me whilst I was helping with the refuelling and said 'Say, I didn't know you guys still flew B.24's. My reply from the top of the wing is quite unprintable.

He continues:

> A quick after-flight and a shower later saw four of us off to Hamilton for a night out on the town, it gave me the strangest feeling to be in the High Street looking at

English Policemen, red letter boxes and have all about you talking American. Weird, that's what it was. We staggered back at about four in the morning to find that the wind had reached storm force and all the aircraft had been moved around into the wind yet again and tied down securely. one of the few occasions I didn't get to play 'Musical Aeroplanes !' The airport the following day was a bit of a mess, one or two of the civilian aircraft were sitting on their tails and one had gone completely over the sea wall, a total write-off.

Tommy Tucker, one of the engine fitters, had his moment when the Safety Raiser he was working on around an engine took off in the general direction of the sea wall, we had forgotten to lock all the feet down. There we were in hot pursuit trying to grab the Raiser before it ran into rough ground with tools and bits flying everywhere. Tommy couldn't see the joke after we caught him and to give him his due he did hang on to all the engine panels. Not one was lost, bent or broken. A true engine fitter down to his grubby fingernails ! The aircraft he was working on may have been Bravo.

09.02.68: WR977 departed Bermuda bound for Curacao, the flight lasted 7.10 hours. They arrived at Dr.Albert Plesman airfield sometime during the afternoon. Ron Cole again recalls:

The Britannia bringing all the sonarbuoys out from St.Mawgan was delayed for 24 hours so it gave us all a chance to take time off to take a leisurely look at Wilhelmstad, the main city in the island. The main business quarter and tourist area formed the heart of the town, all very neat and clean and built in the true Dutch colonial style. All the shops and houses appeared to be painted in light, bright colours which looked very smart under the intense sunlight. Wilhelmstad's port was fairly busy with medium-sized oil tankers coming and going from the oil fields of Venezuela. I was a little more than surprised to see the main bridge across the harbour entrance was of the pontoon nature. I was even more surprised to see the local bridge keeper jump into the first pontoon boat, start the engine and proceed to open the bridge by chugging off in a quarter circle with the bridge pivoted on the opposite shore.

11.02.68: The Britannia arrived, and exercising in the Caribbean began. WR977 flew an undetailed 5.30 hour sortie. This was flown in conjunction with the Dutch Grumman S-2a Tracker aircraft, and eight ships led by HMS London and the submarine HMS Walrus.

However after this sortie No.1 engine is recorded as having been changed at 4610.44 airframe hours.

18.02.68: She was in the air for 48 minutes, undetailed but believed to be an airtest.

Tony Davies remembers she also had a 'duff' Viper (probably port)

08.02.68. WR977 tethered down In Bermuda. (via Ron Cole)

during this period. He notes:

> The Old Lady loved the Caribbean, but it was hot, and the poor old Engineer had his work cut out working out WAT limits, can we use water/meth with Vipers? can we use assymetric Vipers? eventually we used water/meth, it about tore the guts out of the engines, and we needed all of Albert Plesman Field's 12,500 feet to get off the ground. The weight reducing drastically by the amount of sweat each of us lost going down the runway !

Returning to Ron Cole's memories:

> Whilst there, we seemed to have our fair share of false alarms, panics and declared emergencies, so much so that the Airport Fire Chief wandered over to me after one such event and said 'You English, you must come back again soon, never have me and my boys had so much practice!'

19.02.68: The three day Flag waving tour to Venezuela was confirmed. Unfortunately Ron Cole spent his last night reparing a 'sheared generator drive' on one of the aircraft. It is not known which of the three ladies spoilt his plans for a night out, but he says a nice steak in the Airport lounge made up for a lot. They departed in the morning at 0830 hours, Ron remembers:

19.02.68. Taken from Frew Weaver's aircraft XF706 whilst approaching Venezuela, shows WR977 flown by Wing Commander Ryan leading the formation. (via Ron Cole)

That during the morning briefing Wg.Cdr.Ryan decided that 'We would do a bit of formation flying practice to make our arrival look good, and then land in stream formation.' From the back of the room one wag was heard to ask 'Oh you mean one a week Sir?'

The set up for the flight was that the CO would take the lead aircraft 'BRAVO'. Flt.Lt.Weaver would fly on his left and be in the right hand seat for obvious reasons flying 'ECHO'. Flt.Lt.Terry Earl would fly on the CO's right in 'FOXTROT'. Terry Earl in his original article states 'A rather sweaty trip began.'

You're damn right it was, Terry, but not because of the heat ! In my ignorance I stood next to Fred Weaver taking photo's of the formation closing up on the leader, all went well and good whilst flying in a straight line but when a 'gentle turn to the left' was called I thought the end of the world was at hand. I won't say fred's eyeballs came out on stalks but mine certainly did ! I have this mental image, even today, of 'BRAVO' going over the top of us and being able to confirm that most of the 'forty thousand rivets flying in loose formation' are in the bomb doors ! We never really did get our act together after that, but our arrival at Maiquetia Airfield had all the aircraft in the same part of the sky at the same time.

They landed 1.15 hours later and the flag waving tour began which Tony Davies calls 'All parties and armed escorts !' The AOC gave a brief press conference and the detachment left the Shackletons at the coastal airfield and drove up to the capital Caracas. Ron Cole states:

The hospitality of our hosts was second to none, the Sergeant's Mess was what can only be termed as 'palatial'....life just seemed to be one round of sight seeing trips and official functions, although I am sure we did some flying in between.

According to records WR977 remained on the ground until they left on the 21st but Flt.Lt.Earl's crew flew two demonstration flights, probably in 'FOXTROT'.

The city was said to be beautiful and Ron Cole remembers 'I couldn't get over the fact that the city was so cool, but being surrounded by mountains, and like Nairobi, being at great altitude, would explain it all.'

Flt.Lt.Weaver, Captain of XF706 recalls their arrival:

We overflew Maiquetia Airfield in formation before peeling off to land one behind the other. There was quite a large reception party. There is always a lot to do on these occasions and I did not see the departure of either the CO or the AOC and other crews. Eventually my crew were all on board a coach and I had a staff car to myself. As we left the airfield I was aware that we had acquired a 'V' shaped formation of Motorcycles being an escort.

I was very surprised by all this and looking behind, my crew were following in their coach. We travelled up into the mountains along a very modern road. On the outskirts of Caracas there were visible signs of extreme poverty, but in the city itself it was all very different. My little convoy kept going throughout at a constant speed; when we approached a set of traffic lights showing a red light, the motorcycle escort

WR977 banks away from the CARIBEX formation. (via Ron Cole)

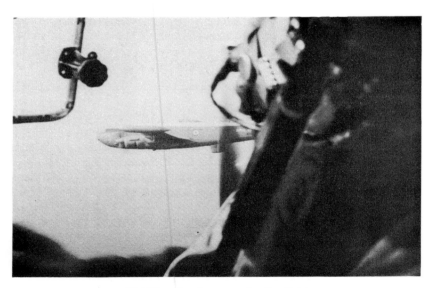

WR977 in close formation. (via Ron Cole)

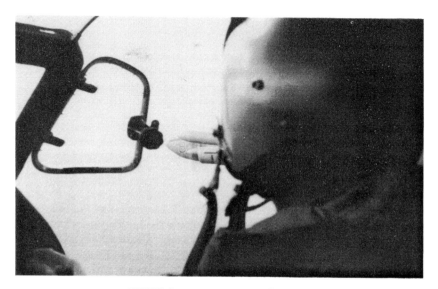

WR977, Bravo even closer. (via Ron Cole)

*The CARIBEX detachment, now in loose formation overflying Caracas, Venezuela.
(via Ron Cole)*

97

shot in front and stopped the crossing traffic. After this had happened several times we came to another crossing where all the lanes were blocked by the waiting traffic. We still pressed on through a gap in the walled flower beds in the centre of the road to find ourselves hurtling on against the traffic flow which was parted to pass either side of us by our escort. We eventually arrived at a Premier Hotel, 'The Tomanaca', which was to be our base for the next few days.

During our three day stay, we were hosted at a Cocktail Party at the Venezuelian Air Force Club. It was really a Palace, with high ceilings, chandeliers, wide stairs, plenty of gold leaf displayed and expensive carpets. We were served with glasses of whisky and ice by Flunkies in the traditional dress of breeches and wearing wigs. One of the other crews flew a demonstration flight taking some senior Venezuelans with them. Whilst this was going on, we were taken up to the top of one of the mountains which surround Caracas by cable car. At the top there is an ice rink. We were all taken to a Venezuelian Air Base about 70 miles from Caracas, where we attended a Cocktail Party before an official lunch. On the way back we stopped and walked into a Sugar Plantation. We all attended another Cocktail Party at the British Consul's Residence, at which were people from the various Embassies in Caracas.

21.02.68: Sadly all good things come to an end, and after the three days were up it was time to go. Ron Cole: 'Please let there be a massive Mag. drop on any of the engines and we've got no spare plugs !' No such luck ! The trip back to the airfield was not without incident. The bus driver took a wrong turning and we ended up going down onto the motorway the wrong way. With that and without further ado one of the Air Force guards...was out of the door and onto the road, he put his hand up and the traffic came to a blinding halt. After much fiddling about we were facing the right way and we were rejoicing.

Just before the CO climbed aboard his aircraft, most likely WR977, he was informed of the birth of his first child, a baby boy. Dave Lawrence after a break from WR977 returned as Co-Pilot, and Tony Davies remained as AEO for the return home. This was a 7.10 hour transit from Maiquetia, Venezuela to Kindley AFB, Bermuda. WR977's captain is unknown, as Wg.Cdr.Ryan flew with Flt.Lt.Weaver in XF706.

22.02.68: WR977 flew from Bermuda into Lajes in the Azores, flying time 9.50 hours.

23.02.68: The final stage home for WR977 and crew, was an 8.05 hour transit from Lajes to St.Mawgan. They left Fred Weaver back at Lajes with engine trouble on XF706. On WR977's arrival back home No.4 engine and the port Viper were changed.

28.02.68: 45 minutes flown, probably an airtest after an engine change. After which the port undercarriage and port Viper were changed at 4638 airframe hours.

04.03.68: Flt.Lt.Weaver flew '977 with Flg.Off.Kemble and Crew 5 for a Day Mandatory which lasted 2.25 hours, and made a 3 engine Day landing and 4 engine and asymmetric NDB and ILS approaches. 45 minutes were simulated instrument flying.

13. & 15.03.68: 16.40 hours flown, after the 15th No.4 engine was changed at 4657.50 airframe hours. She did not fly again until the 28th.

28.03. - 05.04.68: 33.10 hours flown in six undetailed sorties.

10.04.68: Flt.Sgt.Hosie returned to '977 after a break from her, due to the birth of his son. He flew a 2.25 hour Day Mandatory sortie with Flt.Lt.Harris. Total flying time for 'Bravo' on this date was 8.55 hours.

12.04.68: Flt.Lt.Weaver again flew with Crew 5 and Flg.Off.Kemble for O.T. and Day Bombing. 9.00 hours flown in total - 5.45 hours Day and 3.15 hours Night, with 30 minutes simulated instrument flying.

14.04.68: 8.15 hours no details.

25.04.68: Ian Mallen flew on WR977 for the first time, as AEOp, with Crew 5 on O.T., a Stage II, Bombing and AMAC Team Trials. They flew 7.15 hours Day and 20 minutes Night, with Flt.Lt.Weaver and Kemble and Flt.Sgt.Jock Hosie.(Another captain is noted for this flight by Flt.Lt.Weaver - Sqdn.Ldr.Presnail, a Navigator.

26.04.68: Wg.Cdr.Ryan, OC 42 Squadron flew WR977 for O.T., Vertical Photography and Mandatory flying. The sortie lasted 6.20 hours according to Jock Hosie.

29.04.68: Ian Mallen again flew as AEOp, put this time to John Harris for Pilot Conversion lasting 5.00 hours.

03.05.68: Ian Mallen again flew with Flt.Lt.Harris for a day Transit to Bitteswell, Hawker Siddeley Aircraft (HSA), which lasted 1.20 hours. This was Ian Mallen's last flight in '977, he'd flown 14 hours in just three flights, before being posted to another unit. HSA Bitteswell was to be 'Bravo's' new home for a short time as she was there for modifications. She transferred there under authority MC/A/210.

Due to the problems encountered with the heavy Phase 3 version of the Mk.3 further modifications were required. The worst of these was the Centre of Gravity which was too far back in the airframe and to combat this problem it was decided to remove the lining from the interior of the rear fuselage aft of the galley. The loss of heavy soundproofing meant increased noise, so HSA sprayed a green flock over the inner side of the single aluminium skin. However, as many ex-Viper fit Shackleton crews have vouched, it was not very effective. Some also suggest that the weight removal was too drastic and under certain conditions the CoG could be too far forward.

It is also believed that at this time she was fitted with a Honeywell radar altimeter, to replace the old radio altimeters which wern't particularly compatible with the type. This entailed the removal of the tail skid and the fitting in its place a box containing the altimeter. The instrument itself was fitted on the pilot's instrument panel on the flight deck. This box can be seen on subsequent photographs of the aircraft. Other minor modifications were completed but we have no details of what they were. Whilst there the port Viper was changed at 4734.10 airframe hours.

01.08.68: An undetailed 1.20 hour flight believed to be a transfer back to St.Mawgan, under Authority MC/A/377. She was officially handed back to 42 Squadron on this date at 4734.10 airframe hours.

19. & 21.08.68: Undetailed flights, approx. 7 hours flown.

24.08.68: Flt.Lt.Weaver took her up for the first detailed flight after her mods. This was a flight with Sqdn.Ldr.Ilsley as first Pilot and Crew 5 from St.Mawgan to Gibraltar.

25.08.68: Flying for 7.40 hours Sqdn.Ldr.Ilsley, Flt.Lt.Weaver and crew

WR977 of 42 Squadron, believed to have been taken in May 1968. (via R.B. Ashworth)

took WR977 from Gib. to Luqa, carrying out Day Bombing en route.

26. - 29.08.68: No details other than flying hour total, 14.45 hours.

30.08.68: It was around this date that WR977 is often noted as having transferred units, although there appears to be no evidence to support this. Flt.Lt.Weaver took over as WR977's First Pilot again, with his usual Co-Pilot Flg.Off.Kemble and Crew 5 for Exercise Cavern. A 9.30 hour flight but no details of the exercise itself.

31.08. & 01.09.68: No details for 18.00 hours flown.

03.09.68: Sqdn.Ldr.Ilsley as pilot, again with Fred Weaver and Crew 5 for the start of the return journey to St.Mawgan. This sortie was a transit from Luqa to Gibraltar with Admiral Bayly as a passenger. Each pilot flew her for around 3.15 hours, for a total of 6.25 hours.

101

FLYING PROGRAMME

N.B. — This programme is subject to alteration due to weather or Service requirements. Announcements will be made over the public address system.

Item No.	Time (Local)	Event
1	1320	Take-off by RN Wessex with 22 Air Despatch Squadron Free Fall Parachute Team.
2	1338	Take-off by four Shackleton Mk 2 Phase 3 aircraft of RAF Coastal Command.
3	1341	Streamer from Wessex to determine Wind Velocity.
4	1342 — 1352	Fire fighting and crash rescue demonstration by a H43B helicopter of the USAF.
5	1353 — 1354	Fly past by the Four Shackleton Mk 2 Phase 3 Formation.
6	1355 — 1359	Parachuting demonstration by 22 Air Despatch Squadron Free Fall Team.
7	1400 — 1409	Take-off, display and landing by a Spitfire from Coltishall.
8	1409½	Landing by RN Wessex at No. 22 Squadron—Hangar 405.
9	1410 — 1420	Display of formation aerobatics by the "Rough Diamonds" of the Royal Navy.
10	1420½ — 1425½	Display by a Britannia of Air Support Command.
11	1427 — 1431	Take-off and display by a Buccaneer of the Royal Navy.
12	1432 — 1434	Take-off and Photographic run by a Hunter P.R.10.
13	1434½ — 1439½	Display by a VC10 of Air Support Command.
14	1441 — 1446	Take-off and display by a Gannet of the Royal Navy.
15	1447 — 1453½	Solo Aerobatic display by a Hunter of Strike Command.
16	1454	Hunter P.R.10 lands.
17	1455	Run in and break by Shackleton formation of the M.O.T.U.
18	1456	Take off by a Shackleton Mk 3 Phase 3 of No. 42 Squadron.
19	1457 — 1502	Landing by Shackleton formation of the M.O.T.U.
20	1503 — 1505	Display by an Andover of Air Support Command.
21	1505½ — 1508	Display by four F104G aircraft of the Royal Danish Air Force.
22	1509	Landing by a Fouga Magister of the Royal Belgian Air Force.
23	1511 — 1517	Take-off and display of synchronised aerobatics by 2 Chipmunks of the Bristol University Air Squadron. Aircraft will land to refuel.
24	1518 — 1523	Display by a Hercules of Air Support Command.
25	1524 — 1529	Display by a Belfast aircraft of Air Support Command.
26	1530 — 1535	Display by a formation of Three Dominie aircraft of Training Command.
27	1536	Take-off by four Jet Provost aircraft of Training Command.
28	1536½ — 1541½	Display by a Victor Mk 2 BS of Strike Command.
29	1542 — 1546	Auto land demonstration and display by a Comet aircraft of the Ministry of Technology.
30	1547 — 1555	Formation aerobatic display by four Jet Provost aircraft of Training Command.
31	1556 — 1600½	Display by a Nimrod aircraft of Hawker Siddeley Aviation.
32	1601 — 1606	Display by a Vulcan aircraft of Strike Command.
33	1607 — 1615	Solo aerobatic display and landing by a Gnat aircraft of Training Command. Aircraft lands to refuel.
34	1616	Jet Provost formation aerobatic Team lands aircraft to refuel.
35	1617 — 1621	Display by a Sea Vixen of the Royal Navy.
36	1622	Take-off by the Spitfire for display at St. Athan.
37	1623	Take-off by RN Wessex for 2nd Parachute display.
38	1625	Take-off of the "Rough Diamonds" for the display at St. Athan.
39	1626 — 1636	Take-off, aerobatic display by a Fouga Magister of the Royal Belgian Air Force before departure to St. Athan.
40	1637 — 1642	Search and Rescue winching display by a Whirlwind Mk 10 of No. 22 Squadron.
41	1643 — 1650	Take-off and demonstration of a Survival Equipment and Weapon Drop from a Shackleton of No. 42 Squadron.
42	1651 — 1656	Parachuting demonstration by 22 Air Despatch Squadron Free Fall Team.
43	1657 — 1700	Take-off and Display by a Lightning aircraft of Strike Command before return to Wattisham.

STATIC AIRCRAFT DISPLAY

Aircraft	Base
F100	USAF Weatherfield
RF-101	USAF Upper Heyford
F4C	USAF Bentwaters
Vulcan Mk 2 FF	RAF Finningley
Gnat	RAF Valley
Jet Provost	RAF Little Rissington
Varsity	RAF Little Rissington
Canberra B18	RAF Laarbruch
Lightning	RAF Marham
Victor Tanker	RAF Wattisham
Meteor T7	RAF Little Rissington
Whirlwind Mk 10	RAF St Mawgan
Wasp	RNAS Culdrose
Shackleton Mk 3	RAF St Mawgan

RAF St. Mawgan At Home Day September 14th 1968, see items 18 and 41. (Reproduced from the Display Programme)

04.09.68: With the same crew and Admiral Bayly, '977 was flown on to Lisbon, with each pilot flying her for a little over an hour. The daily total was 2.15 hours. This must have been where they dropped the Admiral off as they left for Cornwall the same day without him, arriving home some 5.45 hours later. Again each pilot had equal time at the controls, 1.00 hours flying was made at night. After her arrival back a new No.3 engine was fitted at 4811.40 airframe hours. She did not fly again for almost a week.

10.09.68: 3.55 hours flown, undetailed.

14.09.68: This was RAF St.Mawgan's AT HOME Air Display. The flight log shows 1.40 hours flown, although details are not known. However the Display Programme records a 1456 hour 'take off by a 42 Squadron Shackleton Mk.3', and later from 1643 to 1650 hours a 'take off, demonstration of survival equipment and weapons drop from a 42 Squadron Shackleton Mk.3.' It is believed that WR977 was one of these aircraft.

16. & 17.09.71: 17.45 hours flown.

19.09.68: WR977 was flown by Fred Weaver and crew for a Distant Support sortie on Exercise Silver Tower, it lasted 7.30 hours Day and 1.30 hours Night. 2.30 hours were actual instrument flying and Flt.Lt.Weaver made QGH and GCA approaches. Further details on the Exercise are not available, although Chris Ashworth notes that it was a Sub-Air Exercise.

20. & 21.09.68: No details, 20.20 hours flown. After the 21st No.2 engine and No.3 front prop. were changed. She was obviously given a 45 minute airtest on 02.10.68 after which No.4 front prop. was also changed. Airframe hours were around 4864.

07.10.68: This flight and many others from now on are detailed by a Navigator (Navigator Leader) on the unit at the time Sqdn.Ldr. P.S.Cole, brother of Ron Cole a Ground Technician on the squadron who we encountered earlier. Flt.Lt.Baugh was the pilot for this sortie with Dave

WR977 captured after the 1968 Mods., and with rescue arrow markings, she could now be with 203 Squadron. (Museum Collection)

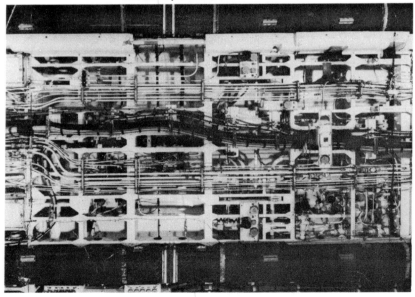

An unusual view of WR977's Bomb Bay. (Museum Collection)

Lawrence as his Co-Pilot, and Flt.Sgt.Hosie as Engineer for a 6.15 hour transit to Gibraltar (1 hour Night flying). This was the first stage of a lengthy detachment to Malta in order that the unit could combat the build up of Russian activity in the area. As noted earlier this may be where the confusion over the often noted transfer to 203 Squadron may have occurred. 203 were waiting and preparing to move to Luqa permanently, 42 were merely covering until they got there, although only part of the unit was detached. She was never handed over according to her records, and 42 Squadron were still operating her thus no evidence can be traced to show a unit change. For some of their time in Malta, 42 had to operate out of Hal Far due to runway resurfacing at Luqa. At Hal Far take off weights were restricted, and even when 203 Squadron arrived it was a short time before they could move on to Luqa.

From log book entries the following aircraft appear to have been on the detachment WR974, WR977, WR978, WR984, XF706 and XF707.

08.10.68: The same crew as for the previous transit now go on to Luqa in 4.15 hours Day and 2.00 hours Night.

09.10.68: Flt.Sgt.Hosie records a 5.30 hour Mandatory sortie with Flt.Lt.Baugh. Exactly half Day and half Night.

23.10.68: 11.45 hours flown, no details.

08.11.68: Dave Lawrence notes an 'Airtest and Mandatory' sortie. He didn't record a flight time but WR977's daily total was 7.00 hours.

09.11.68: Sqdn.Ldr.Cole records a sortie on Exercise 'EDEN APPLE', with Flt.Lt Baugh, flying for 11.25 hours. This would seem to be the same flight as noted by Dave Lawrence as a Surveillance sortie, during which they were diverted to a SAR search. He did not note the details, and this was his last flight in WR977.

'EDEN APPLE' is noted by Chris Ashworth as 'a large scale NATO Exercise in the Mediterranean that involved the US Sixth Fleet and all the maritime forces in the area.'

11.11.68: Fred Weaver and crew flew '977 on Exercise 'EDEN APPLE' for a SURVEX lasting 10.05 hours, including 2.00 hour Night. They made NDB and GCA approaches. Total flying for that day was 11.25 hours, so a further flight may have taken place, albeit quite a short one.

12. & 14.11.68: 19.20 hours flown, but no details.

15.11.68: Flt.Lt.Weaver and Kemble with Crew 5 flew a further 'EDEN APPLE' Day and Night sortie, this time on Close Support, and they had one confirmed Submarine contact. 7.15 hours Day and 4.15 hours Night.

17.11.68: 11.15 hour sortie, no details.

19. - 21.11.68: Flt.Lt.Weaver flew Bravo to Naples, he explains:

Whilst on a 42 Squadron detachment to Luqa, Malta I was sent to Naples flying WR977 to lead a flypast over the parade marking the inauguration ceremony of the new NATO Command Headquarters at Naples. We arrived during a thunderstorm. Because of the poor visability, a matter of yards, caused by the torrential rain, we were eventually located by a 'follow me car', which guided us to a car parking area in front of tha main building. Since no one took any notice of our arrival, I ran out into the building and after a time found an American Officer, who made a few telephone calls and introduced me to an enlisted man who he said would drive my crew and I to our accommodation. (We knew not where.)

This man took me to the rear of the building where we set off in an American Bus. After we had travelled a short distance I suggested that as we were in an aircraft manoeuvering area a little bit more care should be exercised. His reply was. 'Gee Sir, I have never driven a bus before but when my officer tells me to drive a bus, I drive a bus!' Such is life. Having collected my crew we set off away from the airfield and were soon in the centre of Naples, where a vehicle in front of us was involved in a minor traffic accident. This produced a crowd, whilst the two drivers waved their arms and shouted at each other. It was a few minutes before we were able to proceed.

After the storm had abated somewhat another 42 Squadron crew from Luqa captained by Flt.Lt.Pat.Patterson landed. They arrived at our hotel much later. It seems as though they had much the same experience with transport as we did, except that their bus was itself involved in a traffic accident in Naples.

The next day we attended a briefing. I was to lead a formation with an American Neptune in No.2 position and the other Shackleton in No.3 position. Behind would be a Squadron of Italian Tracker aircraft and also several Squadrons and Flights of various types of helicopters. I was to start my run from Capri leaving at a specified time, height and speed and was told that all the other aircraft would formate on me as I crossed the Bay of Naples. This briefing was followed by a rehearsal. I kept my fingers crossed.

On the day all the aircrews attended a meteorology briefing which was given by a Senior Italian Air Force Officer wearing a gold braided hat and several rows of medal ribbons. He spoke in Italian. - When we left a junior Italian officer said to me, what he was trying to tell you was, that if it did not rain it would be fine. After the event and much to my surprise I was told that all the aircraft were in their correct positions and that the flypast was exactly what was required.

One fills in one's log books some time later especially when the entries relate to flights abroad. It can happen that whilst doing this one can be distracted by perhaps a telephone call. In my entries recording the Naples flights the date for the rehearsal flight is wrong. it should be the 20th November. Also, it was a long time ago, but I do not recall having any reason to change aircraft or that I actually did so. I have recorded that I flew XF730 on the actual day of the inauguration ceremony. It is just possible that I made a mistake and that it was WR977 that led the flypast. A quick check of the log books belonging to the crew members of each aircraft should clear up this point.

The flying times for those trips were as follows:

19.11. Luqa to Naples, 2.10 hours.

20.11. Practice flypast and formation flying, 1.15 hours.

21.11. Formation flying and flypast at Naples then return to Luqa, 4.15 hours flying.

This was Flt.Lt.Fred Weaver's last flight in '977 on 42 Squadron, he'd flown her for 191.45 hours, and over the two tours on which he flew her, he totalled 420.55 hours in her.

23.11.68: No details but around 7.30 hours flown.

27.11. - 09.12.68: Six flights making 40 flying hours, After which No.1 front and No.3 front and rear props. were changed.

30.12.68: 3.55 hours flown after which No.3 engine was swapped and she didn't fly until just into the new year.

03. - 08.01.69: 38.35 hours flown on four sorties. She didn't fly from the 8th to 10th due to a new No.3 front prop. being fitted.

10.01.69: 18.10 hours recorded. No.2 engine was replaced after this flight, along with the starboard Viper, at 5080 airframe hours.

14.01.69: 35 minutes flown, probably an Airtest.

18.01. 22.02.69: Nine flights undetailed, 88.50 flying hours. No.'s 1 and 4 engines were changed at 5167 airframe hours. By now 203 Squadron had moved to their new permanent base of Luqa.

28.02.69: 3.45 hours flying, no details.

03.03.69: Flt.Sgt.Hosie and Sqdn.Ldr.Cole flew with Flt.Lt.Scobbie for a sortie on Exercise 'Razor Sharp', 7.00 hours Day and 1.40 hours Night. Sqdn.Ldr.Cole notes '1 submarine certified.'
Around this time the 42 Squadron Malta detachment returned to St.Mawgan.

04.03.69: An undetailed 6.00 hour sortie after which at around 5185 hours No.3 engine was changed.

06. - 12.03.69: 39.50 hours flown in 5 sorties. After the 7th a service extension was given of 125 hours.

14.03.69: This was Jock Hosie's last flight in WR977, with Wg.Cdr.Ryan for a transit from St.Mawgan to Lisbon, but after 45 minutes Day and 6.00 hours Night they had to RTB due to a compass fault.
Flt.Sgt.Hosie had flown 236.45 hours in WR977 in almost three years, and he had been with her for many interesting and often most famous sorties during that period. However, this was not to be the last time he would have close contact with the aircraft, he was to remain closely associated with his beloved WR977.

19. - 21.03.69: Three flights for 31.25 hours, no details.

24.03.69: This was Flt.Lt.Brian Woodward's (Navigator) first flight in '977. Flt.Lt.Calvert was the pilot on a WESTAXE of 8.35 hours, this was mainly flown at Night.
As she was due for a Minor Service at 5273.22 airframe hours, after this sortie she didn't fly again until May. The starboard undercarriage and

radius rod (18.04.69) was changed, along with the nose undercarriage (12.05.69) and No.4 rear prop.

13.05.69: 1.20 hours flown, no details but likely to be an airtest.

16.05.69: 8.40 hours flown no details, after which No.3 front prop. and engine were changed at 5283.30 airframe hours.

20.05.69: Sqdn.Ldr.Cole records a flight with Flg.Off.Palmer for an ECM Trial of 7.45 hours duration.

21.05. - 19.06.69: No details for 11 flights, totalling 80.50 hours.

20.06.69: P.S.Cole again records a flight with Flg.Off.Palmer taking '977 to Ballykelly for a 'TORPEVAL' (Torpedo Evaluation), 2.15 hours flying.

21.06.69: Return transit form Northern Ireland to St.Mawgan, the 'TORPEVAL' was cancelled, WX was u/s, i.e. Bad weather unsuitable for torpedo dropping.

22. - 30.06.69: No details for five flights, a total of 34.25 hours.

14

LOAN TO 206

In the previous undetailed section a note in the Flight Log 'To Kinloss' notes the probable transit day for the loan.

At this point '977 was loaned to 206 Squadron based at Kinloss, for two months. The reason for the loan has not been identified.

01.07.69: The only detailed flight for this period comes from John Wolff an AEO of 206 Squadron at the time. He flew a 10.35 hour Day sortie on Exercise 'Stong Gale', a SURVEX flown by Flt.Lt.Read.

02.07.69: 1.05 hours undetailed, a note under this trip in the Flight Log indicates the end of a detachment to Machrihanish, and what must be a cumulative total of 24.20 hours. This was almost certainly flown from the 2nd to the 6th, during which the No.2 front prop. was replaced.

08. - 20.07.69: 45.35 hours flown in five flights, after which No.2 engine was changed at around 5485 airframe hours.

28.07.69: Obviously flown over a period, for a cumulative total of 33.05 hours.

29.07. - 01.08.69: 27.00 hours flown, undetailed.

01. - 11.08.69: No.1 and 2 rear props. were changed along with all four TU's.

11.08.69: 6.00 hours flown.

15.08.69: An entry here shows a further detachment, this time to Bodo, Norway from where she returned having flown another hourly total of 33.05.

17. - 25.08.69: Six sorties totalling 48.50 hours. Following a flight on the 17th a main undercarriage down lock had to be fitted. After the 25th

No.4 engine was changed at 5655 airframe hours.

29.08.69: An airtest recorded by Sqdn.Ldr.Cole and piloted by Flt.Lt.Retallack. This must have been her return to 42 Squadron, although not noted as returning until the following day and no return transit is logged. Again she is often said to be 'owned' by 203 Squadron from now, and merely loaned to 42 Squadron. No indication of this can be found on her transfer records.

30.08. - 02.09.69: 19.50 hours flown, and a 98 hour service extension was awarded.

02. - 05.09.69: No.1 engine was changed along with No.'s 1 and 4 front props. at 5675.05 airframe hours.

05.09.69: 12.35 hours flown in 3 sorties.

09.09.69: Sqdn.Ldr.Cole flew with Flt.Lt.Retallack and crew for a CASEX and Night Bombing flight of 4.15 hours Day and 4.50 hours Night for a total of 9.05 hours.

11. & 12.09.69: 19.50 hours flown, no details.

16.09.69: P.S.Cole again gives details for a flight on Exercise 'Peacekeeper', this was a SURVEX lasting 10.45 hours all during the daytime, again with Flt.Lt.Retallack.

17. - 21.09.69: Four undetailed sorties for 34.15 hours.

22.09.69: Flt.Lt.Woodward flew in '977 again, this time as Crew Captain, with Flt.Sgt.Taylor as Pilot for Close Support on Exercise 'Peacekeeper', but they were recalled after 4.55 hours. Only 30 minutes of the trip were in daylight.

24.09.69: A service extension of 125 flying hours given, and 10.17 hours flown with no further details.

26.09.69: Sqdn.Ldr.Cole flew in '977 for 8.00 hours on OT with Flt.Lt.Retallack.

29.09. - 01.10.69: No details but 13.00 hours flown.

02.10.69: Brian Woodward (Captain) details 2 flights with Flt.Sgt.Taylor. The flights were Airways to Machrihanish, 2.25 hours, and Airways return to St.Mawgan in 2.05 hours Day and Night flight.

13. - 27.10.69: Six sorties flown, no further details for 56.15 hours. By now 101.00 hours of the service extension had been flown, and 'Bravo' was due for her Major Service at 5858.36 airframe hours. She didn't fly again until February 1970.

15

WR977's LAST MAJOR SERVICE

This service was to be WR977's last Major before she retired. Some details of what was carried out have been recorded from her documentation.

05.12.69: Aiframe Hours 5858.
> NOSE U/C RETRACTING STAYS FITTED.
> MAIN U/C PT. & STBD. DOWN LOCK JACKS FITTED.
> MAIN U/C PT. & STBD. UP LOCK JACKS FITTED.
> PT. MAIN U/C RADIUS ROD FITTED (NIL HRS.)
> STBD. MAIN U/C RADIUS ROD FITTED (NIL HRS.)
> PT. & STBD. ELECTRO-PNEUMATIC VALVE FITTED.
> ALL FLAME SWITCHES REPLACED.
> PT. & STBD. JETTISON VALVES CHANGED.
> PT. & STBD. FUEL VENT VALVES CHANGED.
> PT. & STBD. VIPER PNEUMATIC VALVES CHANGED.
> AILERONS SERVO MOTOR FITTED.
> RUDDER SERVO MOTOR FITTED.
> ELEVATOR SERVO MOTOR FITTED.
> PT. & STBD. ELECTROMATIC VALVE CHANGED.
> PT. MAIN U/C (S/N EHLW 47 M101) FITTED.
> STBD. MAIN U/C (S/N EHLW 47M 57) FITTED.

Dates Unknown:
> No.3 GRIFFON ENGINE 44076/A638138 FITTED.
> No.4 FRONT AND REAR PROPS. FITTED.
> No.3 TU CHANGED.

02.02.70:
> PT. VIPER FITTED VL203032/A669208.
> STBD. VIPER FITTED VL0203004/A658810.

11.02.70: 1.45 hours flown, probably an airtest following Major.

20.02.- 03.03.70: Four flights undetailed, making 34.05 hours in the air. On March 2nd the Stbd. Down Lock on the U/C had to be changed, and on the 3rd No.1 TU had to be changed.

11.03.70: 2.05 hours no details.

11. - 15.03.70: No.2 engine and TU changed.

15.03.70: 50 minute flight undetailed, but most likely an airtest after the engine change.

16.03.70: Brian Woodward was Captain and Flt.Lt.Huscroft the Pilot for an L.R.O.F.E., they landed at Espinho/Ovar in Portugal for a short detachment to carry out exercises with the Portugese, one other Shackleton was also present. The flight was Day 9.15 hours, Night 45 minutes.

18.03.70: WR977 and her detachment crew completed an 8.00 hour SURVEX.

20.03.70: 'Bravo' and crew returned from Espinho to St.Mawgan flying a 6.30 hour transit.

25.03.70: This was Sqdn.Ldr.Cole's last flight in WR977, with Flt.Lt.Retallack, they completed a Naval Co-Op sortie of 9.00 hours Day and 3.05 hours Night. Sqdn.Ldr.Cole had flown 80.55 hours in her.

25.03. - 02.04.70: No.4 TU changed.

02. & 03.04.70: 9.15 hours flown in two sorties.

03. - 09.04.70: No.4 rear prop. changed.

09. - 24.04.70: 63.35 hours flown in six sorties.

27.04.70: Flt.Lt.Woodward captained the crew for this sortie, flown by a Flt.Lt.Leigh, for a 10.40 hour SURVEX, 1.10 hours of which were flown in darkness.

28.04. - 01.05.70: 16.15 hours flown.

01. - 12.05.70: No.2 engine, TU, front prop., and No.1 rear prop. were all changed at 6033.25 airframe hours.

12. - 18.05.70: 20.50 hours flown in three sorties.

18. - 26.05.70: No.2 engine changed.

26.05.70: 2.25 hours flown, no details.

28.05.70: Flt.Lt.Woodward logs another SURVEX and OT lasting 3.30 hours Day and 3.15 hours Night (6.45 hours total), with Flt.Lt.Leigh.

01. - 10.06.70: 9.40 hour undetailed flight.

04.06.70: Sqdn.Ldr.Julian Denham records a 7.00 hour Mandatory Bombing sortie as Pilot of '977, with Flt.Lt.Thomas as his Co-Pilot.
Sqdn.Ldr.Julian Denham recalls on that trip:

Shackleton Mk.3 Phase 3 Viper fit WR977, 4th June 1970, No. 42 Squadron, ex-RAF St. Mawgan.

This was categorisation flight for No. 42 Squadron, together with some continuation training, during which selected members of the Squadron were asked to demonstrate their skills up to their categories. (Coastal - or 18Gp - aircrew had four categories, representing levels of experience and ability). The Standardisation Unit was based at Headquarters No. 18 Group, RAF Northwood in north west London. It consisted of two pilots, one of whom was the Officer Commanding - called the President, myself at that time; two Navigators, a Flight Engineer, and two Air Electronic Officers. All these held 'Training' positions on Squadrons in the Group, and 'A' Categories. (This last qualification permitted them to wear a gold-finished nameplate with the Group crest on their uniforms above their wings). Much cherished. The aim of the Unit was to assess squadron standardisation, and to an extent, standards; this posed a problem to squadron commanders, since they largely selected the aircrew for examination; put up the best, as available, and hide the not-so-good; or bring out the dead wood and hope to expose their failings and thereby improve their training. In all cases, a happy compromise was reached. Our findings were given squadron commanders, and a written report submitted to the AOC.

During the week prior to this flight, the Unit was at Base, compiling a report regarding a visit to No. 120 Sqdn. at RAF Kinloss. On Sunday night we travelled by sleeper train and RAF transport to RAF St. Mawgan. On arrival I visited the Wing

Commander Flying, and the OC No. 42 Sqdn., and the Unit began their series of checks. At this stage these were oral examinations to a set syllabus. Squadrons carried out their own in-house training programmes continually, and our job was to make a check on the quality of this training.

On the 1st and 2nd selected crews were checked in the air. A 10 hour flight, and a 5 hour flight which included an Instrument Rating. Further checks continued on the ground.

On the 4th June myself and my No. 2, Flight Lieutenant Thomas took WR977 for a local flight, to update ourselves, and to make further checks.

A short briefing covered the various aspects. The weather was very good, and the sea was a wonderful blue, but a diversion airfield was arranged as normal, the fuel and bomb load decided, and the radar buoy booked with Mountbatten for radar homings and bombing. From briefing to engine start took about 30 minutes; checks on engines and electronic equipment about 10 minutes for a routine training trip like this, but the usual great interest was taken in magneto 'drops' and the CSUs exercised with warm oil. Then the Vipers were started, take-off clearance obtained from the tower, and a normal take-off made to 4,000 feet, using RW 31, across the cliff top and out over the sea. We returned to overhead St. Mawgan, made a hold for practice, and made an ILS approach, with an overshoot (as they were then called) from 200 feet above the threshold. Then an NDB approach, and out over the sea to the Exercise Area at 1,000 feet. The aircraft was prepared for bombing, and a run made to identify the buoy. Repeated runs followed, to practise the procedures, let the radar operators demonstrate their skills, taking turns at the ASV21. The runs ended in bombing attacks, dropping two 8½ lb practice break-up bombs to simulate a stick of depth charges. The pilots bombed from 100 feet, and the navigators from 250 feet. Occasionally during a pilot attack, I signalled for an engine to fail. This simulated gun-fire from the submarine knocking out an engine, and the exercise was for the handling pilot to identify which was the failed engine, feather the propeller, control the yaw, and none-the-less continue the attack and bomb the submarine.

The convention for 'failing' an engine was for the command pilot to put his hand discretely towards the engineer, exposing the number of fingers for the number of the engine to be failed. Three fingers indicates Number 3 and so on. The engineer then grasped the outstretched fingers, indicating that he knew which engine to fail and then switched off the fuel. Power on that engine was then lost, but indications on the pilots' panel remained normal, and the pilot had to identify the failed engine by yaw. The engineer was not normally permitted to help, although he would see the temperatures and pressure change.

Having assessed on which side the failure was (yaw, corrected by rudder), an appropriate throttle was closed. More yaw - not that one; no more yaw, probably that one. RPM lever through the feathering gate, press the feathering button, switch off the fuel. But .... be careful! Get the right engine. 6 eyes are watching like hawks. By 1970, a Shackleton on three was OK; but a Shackleton on two at a couple of hundred feet was a Shackleton in trouble.

116

For Shackleton old hands, I add here that the characteristics of the CSU could also be used to identify engine failures - but great care had always to be exercised.

To return to bombing submarines:

Only the first and last bombs of the stick were actually dropped for practice. Attacks were also photographed, and assessed later by the Nav Sections.

The attack navigator had a bombsight - a help or a hindrance? But how did the pilots do it? Just a feeling at the time that now was the moment to press the tit. IAS, the conditions, the target just slipping under the nose, all these and a feeling. Each squadron kept a bombing ladder which you strove to climb.

Bombing completed, we clear to the north. The WOP has been in contact with MHQ Mountbatten throughout, and sends a report. So far, coffee, sandwiches and soup have been served - it's energetic work! Now lunch proper is fitted in (Chicken, potatoes and peas) but work continues. Detection procedures, W/T reporting, fuel management etc. are all being checked by the Unit. A new procedure for photographing ships has just been introduced and the Cat Board is tasked to discover how this is working. The aim is to gain maximum intelligence with the minimum number of passes by the ship. Anyone with an hour or so can get some good pictures, but can you do it to order in just a few minutes? We find a suitable ship moving up the Bristol Channel by radar, manoeuvre to cross her bow and down one side, climb to look down on the decks, across the stern, and down the other side. The port beam window is open and manned by the signaller photographer and the pilot flying gives a running commentary to warn him for the shots.

Now a spot of low flying: I mean really low. A touch on the stick and we've all had it. We're in amongst the waves, eyes glued to the radio altimeter. A necessary exercise for shadowing ships. We climb a few hundred feet, perhaps with relief, pass Hartland Point, Bude Haven and we are running into Newquay and climbing to join the St. Mawgan circuit. We finish the flight with some roller landings, and I am keen to demonstrate the use of the autopilot for instrument approaches. Autopilots then were not what they are today and lots of technique was required to get them to function helpfully, particularly with elevator trim.

Everything is fine on this flight, but it is in our nature to hold a debrief and pass on to the Squadron crew members what we can.

The next day, we hold a full debrief at the Squadron. Points and counter-points. A meeting with the Station Commander and we are on our way home, a long journey. During the following week, we will put together our formal report, sort out any problems arising, but on the Squadron they are saying 'Well, that's the end of them for another year!' But no flying can be efficient or safe without continual training and checking and that's as true today as it was then.

08.06.70: 6.55 hours flown, no details.

08. - 11.06.70: No.2 engine changed along with its T.U. at 6087 airframe hours.

11. - 30.06.70: Four undetailed flights totalling 23.20 hours.

01.07.70: Flt.Lt.Leigh was to fly a CASEX C2 in '977, but they had to RTB because she misbehaved and went U/S. The flight only lasted 1.05 hours and Flt.Lt.Woodward logs that they eventually did the sortie in XF707.

03.07.70: An undetailed sortie of 9.25 hours.

07.07.70: This was Brian Woodward's last flight in the airframe, with Flt.Lt.Leigh they carried out OT for 5.10 hours. He'd flown over 66.00 hours in her. A further flight must have taken place, bringing the daily total to 12.20 hours.
    This was WR977's last detailed flight before leaving the Squadron and the Country.

09. - 23.07.70: Three sorties flown totalling 28.30 hours with no details.

23.07. - 07.08.70: A new No.4 engine fitted at 6161.08 airframe hours.

07.08.70: 1.05 hour flight probably an airtest, and her last trip with the unit.

Finishing off this section, Chris Inward, an Air Signaller on 42 Squadron who flew in WR977 several times between 1966 and 1969, recalls an incident for which no date is recorded:

> This involved the pilots inadvertently managing to shut both engines down on one side while doing circuits at close to maximum landing weight.
> As you probably know, the old lady, in its Phase 3 version, didn't fly very well on two. This was early in Phase 3 days before the Viper variable throttle facility, so they were only used for take-offs. Fortunately, The Flight Engineer, Master Engineer Ken Isborne, realised what had happened as we careered across the airfield sideways, with the pilot trying to keep it straight, and the altimeter unwinding somewhat quicker than desired.
> Fortuitously, while Ken was lighting up both Vipers, the flight path took us down into the valley between St.Mawgan and St.Eval, and subsequently over the top of

married quarters at St.Eval, probably more by chance than any input from the pilots.

The Vipers came good very quickly, and then the Griffons were brought back into use, and from being on two at (less than) zero feet, were on six at about 5000 feet, enjoying a (very) nervous fag apiece, even those who didn't smoke ! As the Captain said afterwards, 'I wanted to get home early tonight, but not with the rest of the crew, and the aircraft !'

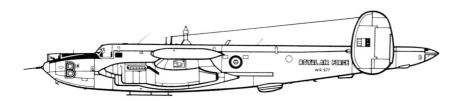

16

WR977 BECOMES 'THE MALTESE ANGEL'

08.08.70: No flight, but '977 was officially handed over on paper to 203 Squadron at Luqa, Malta, under authority MC/A/48/70 at 6162.13 airframe hours.

09.08.70: WR977 made the transit, flown by Flt.Lt.Mike Clegg of 203 Squadron to Luqa of 6.45 hours. Her nose code was to remain the same, 'BRAVO', and she became the oldest Mk.3 on the Squadron at the time.

13.08.70: An undetailed sortie of 30 minutes only.

21.08.70: Her first detailed flight with her new unit was an 'Air Check' flown by Flt.Lt.'s Mike Clegg and Ted Buddin, this was after the fitment of a new Port rudder which is recorded as having been fitted that day at 6169.30 airframe hours.

27.08.70: Signaller Des Proud logs an Air Check, SURVEX, and OT sortie with Flt.Lt.Clegg, which is also noted by the Co-Pilot for that and the previous sortie Flt.Lt.Buddin. 4.30 hours Day and 1.35 hours Night.

02.09.70: 4.30 hours flown undetailed.

09.09.70: No flight, but the nosewheel steering motor was changed.

12.09.70: No flight, nosewheel U/C changed.

16.09.70: Flt.Lt.Bryn Wayt met '977 for the first time, flying with Flt.Lt.Ladbrooke as his Co-Pilot, they set out for OT, Skids and Stage II. Bryn Wayt notes on this flight:

> My first flight with her - 40 minutes airborne! DNCO (Duty Not Carried Out) because the nosewheel would not retract. I cannot remember if we had to get rid of fuel to get to MLW or we did something in between, to pass those 40 minutes.

They completed 15 minutes simulated instrument flying and made a

GCA and an ILS approach. Nosewheel trouble due to nosewheel change on the 12th? Another flight was made at some time on this date as the daily total was 4.30 hours.

18.09.70: 5.30 hours in Flight Log, no details.

22.09.70: 9.25 hours logged, 5.00 hours of which were flown by Flt.Lt.Wayt for OT making five landings, and 45 minutes simulated instrument flying. Flt.Lt.Wayt notes:'Nothing in my log-book after those 5 hours - must have behaved herself pretty well after a naughty start.'

After this flight WR977 went for a Minor Service and did not fly for a month. No.'s 2 and 3 engines, all four TU's , No's 1, 2, 3 front and 2 and 3 rear props. were changed during the service. Also on October 12th the Stbd. Main U/C was changed.

20.10.70: An undetailed 1.45 hour flight, probably an Air Check.

22.10.70: Des Proud and Flt.Lt.Buddin (Co-Pilot) record a flight with Flt.Lt.Clegg as Pilot for OT and Mandatory flying. This sortie only lasted 45 minutes and Ted Buddin notes that an asymmetric landing was made due to low oil pressure.

26.10.70: Flt.Lt.Wayt logs a flight with Sqdn.Ldr.Ken Appleford as his Co-Pilot, a Flight Check and ¼ Asym. check which lasted 40 minutes. Bryn Wayt notes a ¼ Asym. check as 'The quarterly asymmetric check-ride. One engine is shut down for training.'

No.1 engine changed at 6205 airframe hours.

28.10.70: Back with Des Proud and Ted Buddin who again flew with Flt.Lt.Clegg as 1st Pilot for an 8.30 hour Surveillance Exercise.

03. & 07.11.70: 19.05 hours flown but undetailed.

08.11.70: 'Dicky' Henderson made his first flight on WR977, as her Engineer, with Flt.Lt.Whitome, on Exercise 'Lime Jug' which occupied the Squadron that month. This sortie lasted 7.00 hours Day and 3.35

hours Night, for a total of 10.35 hours.

12. & 13.11.70: Two flights undetailed for 18.55 hours.

25.11.70: Ted Buddin records an IRT sortie with Ken Appleford as Captain. They flew for 2.10 hours, Ted Buddin notes 'engine failed on finals.' The total flown on this date was 3.25 hours, therefore another sortie took place - presumably earlier in the day. The result of the engine failure, obviously No.2 as there was a No.2 engine change at 6266 airframe hours which meant she was grounded until the end of the month.

30.11.70: 1.20 hour flight, probably an airtest, a problem may have occurred as afterwards No.4 engine was changed. This was a new engine with nil hours run.

04.12.70: This was intended as a Crew Training sortie flown by Flt.Lt.Clegg and Buddin, and Signaller Des Proud. However, Ted Buddin and Des Proud note a 'Hydraulic Leak' causing a 'Total Hydraulic Failure' causing them to RTB after 50 minutes. As can be seen during this period '977 misbehaved rather a lot.

10.12.70: She flew an undetailed 4.50 hour sortie.

11.12.70: This was the first time '977 was flown by Flt.Lt.Phil Zarraga, for a 3.25 hour Training sortie with Flt.Lt.Wight-Boycott as his Co-Pilot. She appears also to have flown another 4.00 hours on this date.

17.12.70 - 19.01.71: Four sorties totalling 22.20 hours undetailed. After a flight on January 7th, No.3 TU was changed.

21.01.71: Flt.Lt.Bryn Wayt Captained '977 with Flt.Lt.Dave Ladbrooke in the right-hand seat for OT and Mandatory. Flt.Lt.Wayt notes:'She obviously likes me - 8.05 hours carrying out Operational Training and Mandatory Training. All went perfect - DCO.'
  He made a GCA and PAR, and 1 hour Simulated Instrument flying, and a flapless landing with her.

25. & 26.01.71: 3.25 hours undetailed.

27.01.71: Des Proud flew with Sqdn.Ldr.Appleford for an L.R.O.F.E. which lasted 7.00 hours Day and 2.45 hours Night.

29.01.71: 8.15 hours undetailed.

02.02.71: Ted Buddin flew with Flt.Lt.Jarvis for a 3.35 hour Crew Training sortie.

04.02.71: Des Proud flew with Flt.Lt.Clegg for 5.15 hours (2.30 hours at Night) OT and Mandatory flying. Service extension of 125 hours authorised.

06.02.71: This was a Royal SAR sortie logged by her Co-Pilot Ted Buddin, and she was flown by Flt.Lt.Jarvis. Ted Buddin's notes for the 6.40 hour sortie were:'Charles and Anne to Kenya. We only covered the flight over the Med. sorry to say.'
It is known WR977 patrolled between the French and North African coasts at 1000 feet, maintaining radio communications between themselves and the Royal VC10.

08.02.71: Flt.Lt.Wayt flew '977 along with Flt.Lt.Ladbrooke, for an L.R.O.F.E., from which they were diverted (DIV DECIM - Decimomannu, Sicily). The sortie lasted 8.00 hours Day and 2.10 hours Night, this included 1.30 hours Simulated Instrument flying and 1.00 hour Actual. Flt.Lt.Wayt gives further details:
> WE CATCH A SUB. This is the first time the old girl and I catch a submarine - our bread and butter. The remarks column says 'USN' so it looks as if we caught an American! They did not tell us there was one in the area at briefing, so it is a good catch. An 'unalerted detection'. Well done radar - beer for my boys down the back!

10.02.71: 6.15 hours flown.

15.02.71: Flt.Lt.Wayt flew 'Bravo' again, but with a Flt.Lt.Johnson in the right-hand seat for an L.R.O.F.E., and 4.5' Recce. Flt.Lt.Wayt notes on this ' 4.5' - this signifies a sortie dropping 4.5' flares that provided illumination of the target - usually of the SAR nature, but could be of an unlit ship / submarine on the surface.'

The sortie lasted 6.30 hours Day, and 4.00 hours Night, of that 2.15 hours were Instrument flying and a GCA & ILS also completed.

17.02.71: Flt.Lt.Zarraga flew '977 with Flt.Lt.Wight-Boycott, for an 8.50 hour Reconnaissance sortie. A further short flight may also have taken place.

24.02.71: Des Proud flew with Flt.Lt.Clegg for a 10.15 hour L.R.O.F.E.

26.02.71: Des Proud flew her again, this time with the Squadron OC Wing Commander Bowyer. He carried out a 9.20 hour sortie on Exercise 'Bellum', 3.20 hours of the trip were at Night.

26.02. - 03.03.71: No.2 engine changed at 6409.05 airframe hours.

03.03.71: Still with Des Proud, '977 was flown for O.T. and Mandatory by Sqdn.Ldr.Appleford for 3.30 hours.

09.03.71: Dicky Henderson flew two sorties in '977 on this day, the first was for a Mandatory flying and OT with Flt.Lt.Whitome for 2.35 hours. The second was with Ken Appleford again for 1.05 hours for an I.R.T. Dicky Henderson notes that:

> on such occasions one pilot would complete his OT and Mandatory flying, and when he'd finished another pilot would climb in and complete his. Other flights were made on this date bringing the total to 8.25 hours.

09. - 17.03.71: No.2 engine changed at 6421 airframe hours, fitted on the 10th, this recon. had run for 594.45 hours.

17. - 22.03.71: 12.10 hours flown undetailed.

22.03.71: Flt.Lt.Zarraga flew with Flt.Lt.Wight-Boycott on a 7.55 hour Reconnaissance sortie.

25.03.71: Flt.Lt.Zarraga and Wight-Boycott flew her on an Anti-

Submarine Exercise, which Flt.Lt.Zarraga notes as: 'With HMS Auriga', flight duration 5.00 hours.

29.03.71: Flt.Lt.Zarraga flew as Co-Pilot to Ken Appleford for a 5.25 hour Anti-Submarine Exercise again in co-operation with HMS Auriga. Flt.Lt.Buddin also logs a 1.00 hour Crew Training sortie on this date, with Flt.Lt.Jarvis. At least one other flight was made as well, as the Daily Flying Time Record shows 7.20 hours.

After these sorties a new No.2 TU and front prop. was fitted.

01.04.71: Des Proud flew with Mike Clegg for a 10.15 hour Day SURVEX. This was Des Proud's last trip in WR977, his total flying hours were 64.30 in 8 months.

05.04.71: Flt.Lt.'s Zarraga and Wight-Boycott again flew a Recce. sortie of 7.15 hours.

17

WHERE RECORDS BEGIN

From this point on some of the aircraft's records and official documentation for day to day operations and serviceability are available, although they are still incomplete. Where possible these details will now be incorporated into each flight. Help in deciphering and explaining how these records work has been given by a man with 40 years of experience of them, Newark Air Museum's Restoration Co-Ordinator W/O David Leggatt (RAF Rtd.). Although he never operated with Shackletons, W/O Leggatt has worked on a vast number of the aircraft in service with the RAF from the mid-1950's to the mid-1980's, including becoming a Crew Chief on Vulcans and a stint leading the Groundcrew of the Battle of Britain Memorial Flight. His expertise has proved invaluable to Newark Air Museum.

This also seems an opportune moment to include some details and memories from one of '977's most regular pilots at this time Flt.Lt.Bryn Wayt, a Master Green pilot of 203 Squadron. He recalls two funny incidents, which are impossible to tie down to a particular trip or aircraft but as he flew her so often are quite likely to have occurred onboard WR977.

Two quickies that spring to mind; the 2nd Navs hat - a smart sort of bonnet - that he used to wear during the longer sorties. There was a certain dislike for the 'thing' amongst some of the crew down the back, so on one sortie it was 'stolen' and thrown out of the beam window! The first I knew of the incident was when I looked back over my shoulder towards the nav table to see why nobody answered a question I had, to find the nav table completely empty. NO NAVS - not a bad thing now and then, but in the middle of the Med you can always do with a nav or two. It transpired there was a running dispute between the two navs and a few other members of my crew. That was the nearest I had to a mutinity on the high seas, or sky! I think we all pitched in and bought him another 'Andy Cap' that was to the liking of everybody concerned.

How far away is that island?
Same Nav as above. 'Andy' was our new '2nd Nav' and like all navs, they took a pride in pin-point navigation out over the sea. Some of the crew thought we should test his navigation self-confidence. The Co-Pilot and I started a little game; we invented this island out to port, and tried to guess the range of the thing (on intercom, so the nav would hear...) we went for 5 miles then 8 miles and a few in-between, then thought the radar man should settle the debate - by this time we could

see poor old 'Andy' double checking all his charts and measuring this and that, and basically going in a spin. Precipitating a frustrated cry, saying there should not be an island out there!! But when radar started to give ranges close to our guesses, 'Andy' got a bit hot under the collar and leapt to his feet to visually check - only to find NO island. Good laughs all round at the expense of the poor old 2nd Nav - he developed to make a fine navigator. Keeping spirits high was a requirement that was never neglected.

Flt.Lt. Wayt also provides a list of the crew he Captained, Crew One.

1.	Captain	Flt Lt Bryn Wayt
2.	Co-Pilot	Flg Off 'Ted' Buddin
3.	1st Nav	Flg Off 'Dave' Bryant
4.	2nd Nav	Flg Off 'Andy' Foster
5.	AEO	Flt Lt 'Russ' Todd
6.	Engineer	MEng 'Benny' Surgeoner
7.	1st Signaller	MAeOp 'Cy' Hesketh
8.	AEop	Sgt 'Ed' Billings
9.	Signaller	Sgt 'Paul' Middleton
10.	AEop	Sgt 'Mike' Pattenden
11.	AEop	Sgt 'Mick' Bossy
12.	AEop	Sgt 'Pete' Williams

07.04.71: 10.05 hrs. undetailed but after which she didn't fly for a month. No details for this gap are given but some records seem to suggest a Primary service, also No.1 Rear Prop. and No.'s 1&4 TU's were changed, and a Magneto change on No.1 Engine.

At the end of the month the RLE's begin (Red Line Entries), or as it is officially called the 'Change Of Serviceability Log'.

The following entries in the log are dated 26/4/71:

NATURE OF UNSERVICEABILITY	RECTIFICATION 'S' = Serviceable
Oil Dilution System Inoperative	System Not To Be Used.
Cabin Humidifying System Inoperative.	A/C Serviceable To Fly With System Inop.

Signs of Rivits Fretting Between Frames 15 & 16 In Bomb Bay.	A/C 'S' To Fly, No Restrictions. - Area Between Frames 15&16 To Be Inspected At Each Primary. All Certified by a Sqdn.Ldr. Grist.
GEE Removed, 02.04.71.	A/C 'S' To Fly With No Gee Facility. Certified bb Flg.Off. Page.
Slight Separation Of Centre Section Skin From Angle At Rear Face Of Front Spar.	
Slight Separation Of Centre Section Skin & Loosening Of Rivits At Angle At Forward & Rear Face Of Rear Spar.	A/C Serv. To Fly Subject To Check Every 28 Days Certified by Sqdn.Ldr. Grinter.
Loose Rivits & Very Slight Separation At Frames 15 & 16 Under Flap Jack Mounting.	
No.3 Heater Flame Stat. For Over heating Switch Mounting Broken Away From Ducting.	New. Duct Req'd. No.3 Heater Rendered Inop. By Removing Fuses & Fitting Dummy Fuses. Certified Sqdn.Ldr. Grinter.
No.3 Engine Life Expired At 1200 Hrs. (6446 A/F Hrs.)	Further Extension of 100 Hrs. Authorised To Fly Until 1300 Engine Hrs. (6546 A/F Hrs.) In Accordance With HQ NEAF. Certified By Sqdn.Ldr. Grinter

20.05.71: 1.05 Hrs. flown, and a Special Weapons Check Carried out and found to be 'Satisfactory'.

25.05.71: Flt.Lt.'s Wayt and Ladbrooke flew '977 for OT and Mandatory. However an Anti-Collision Light was U/S. She flew for 4.35 Hours. Day and 20 minutes Night, including 1.45 hours, Instrument flying, and making 3 landings all GCA & PAR's. However as Flt.Lt. Wayt himself notes:

> I flew her a few times before today without any problems, but today she weeps hydraulics to spoil the day - RTB.

27.05 - 10.06.71: 4 Undetailed sorties totalling 18.45 hours.

14.06.71: Flt.Lt. Zarraga flew '977 on a brief detachment. Flt.Lt. Andy Wight-Boycott was his Co-Pilot again for a Recce to Cyprus, lasting 9.40 hours. On this date, when WR973 was struck off charge, WR977 was the oldest MR.3 Shackleton serving with the Royal Air Force.

17.06.71: Flt.Lt. Zarraga and crew completed a 9.05 hr. 'Recce' in the Aegean.

19.06.71: They return home to Malta, carrying out a further 'Recce' en route, 8.15 hrs.

F.700's

From this point the 'Fitness For Flight and After Flight Certificates' are available and provide more details about flights, even the ones for which there are no sortie details which have to be provided by a member of the crew involved.

24.06.71: The F.700 was filled in by the Chief Technician (C/T) ready for a flight, but she was not accepted and flown.

25.06.71: A Chief Technician signed '977 over to the crew Captain, Flt.Lt. Whitome at 1055 hours. The 'Conditions Affecting Use' of '977 were:

> Stall Warning Check Required After Port Detector Unit Change
> Air Check Required on No.3 Engine after Prop. Change.

DUTY CARRIED OUT

R.A.F. Form 1125A

LIST OF MODIFICATIONS AND SPECIAL TECHNICAL INSTRUCTIONS EMBODIED
OR FULFILLED DURING REPAIR

Certified that...............**VIPER ENGINE.**............................Mark...**203**...No...**VL.203020/668826.**...has been inspected and tested, and is fit for service. *Complete anti-corrosion treatment has been carried out in accordance with the current instructions *Contract No............**KK/H/657/CB.26(a).**.. *Job No.. Total time *flown/run at Contractor's Works or Maintenance Unit..hours.

MODIFICATIONS EMBODIED: **NIL.**

SPECIAL TECHNICAL INSTRUCTIONS FULFILLED:

NIL.   – 2 MAY 1966   **A.D. V.F.F.**

Date......................................   Signed...Inspector I/c (A.I.D.) or C.I.O. (A.I.S.)

*Delete as necessary.   At...... **Hawker Siddeley Aviation Ltd., Langar, Notts.**...............

4/63   107   Wt.52537-BK2709   36000   4/64   KPLtd   G892   (NOTE: Continue overleaf, if necessary.)

AIRCRAFT No. **WR 977**		TYPE **SHACKLETON**				MARK **3**					R.A.F. FORM No. 4817

AIRCRAFT DAILY FLYING TIMES, RECORD

DATE	Hours	Prog. Total	DATE	Hours	Prog. Total	DATE	Hours	Prog. Total	DATE	Hours	Prog. Total	DATE	Hours	Prog. Total
	Bt./fwd.	663.10		Bt./fwd.	772.30		Bt./fwd.	993.35		Bt./fwd.			Bt./fwd.	1300.50
5.4.59	8.20	671.35	12.1.60	8.00	780.30	25.4.60	15.30	1009.05	219.60	13.00	1161.40	22.12.60	7.25	1313.20
23.4.59	5.40	677.16	14.1.60	11.45	792.15	173			239.60	23.00	1184.40	2.1.61	0.10	1313.30
24.4.59	6.30	685.40	12.2.60	65.25	857.40	22.6.60	2.45	1011.50	24.960	11.00	1195.40	4.1.61	4.40	1318.10
4.5.59	9.50	693.26	18.2.60	6.40	864.20	24.6.60	1.05	1012.55	26.960	12.25	1208.05	16.1.61	8.35	1326.45
4.5.59	9.40	703.20	19.2.60	11.00	868.40	28.6.60	12.00	1024.55	28.960	12.00	1220.05	18.1.61	5.00	1331.45
11.5.59	4.00	704.10	18.2.60	3.40	872.20	30.6.60	15.00	1039.55	4.10.60	7.40	1227.45	19.1.61	0.15	1332.00
14.5.59	1.25	705.35	29.2.60	3.05	875.25	4.7.60	4.10	1044.05	7.10.60	5.05	1232.50	20.1.61	5.20	1337.20
2.11.59	0.55	706.30	2.3.60	2.30	877.55	4.7.60	0.30	1044.35	19.10.60	1.50	1234.40	13.2.61	0.50	1338.10
5.11.59	0.45	707.15	4.3.60	8.00	885.55	11.7.60	8.00	1052.35	31.10.60	1.15	1235.55	17.2.61	2.00	1340.10
26.11.59	2.55	709.40	16.3.60	7.55	893.50	13.7.60	10.30	1063.05	9.11.60	10.20	1246.15	21.2.61	11.10	1351.20
27.11.59	1.15	710.25	28.3.60	10.35	904.25	14.7.60	2.00	1065.05	11.11.60	5.05	1251.20	22.2.61	9.20	1310.40
3.12.59	7.00	717.25	30.3.60	8.40	913.05	15.7.60	8.05	1073.10	14.11.60	4.50	1256.10	24.2.61	2.55	1363.35
8.12.59	0.10	719.35	5.4.60	5.15	918.20	20.7.60	9.40	1082.50	16.11.60	6.45	1262.55	1.3.61	10.00	1373.35
9.12.59	7.30	727.05	7.4.60	9.55	928.15	28.7.60	4.50	1087.40	21.11.60	6.25	1269.20	20.3.61	10.20	1583.58
10.12.59	12.10	739.15	8.4.60	9.50	938.05	4.8.60	8.15	1095.25	25.11.60	4.25	1273.45	1.20		1385.15
17.12.59	12.00	751.15	13.4.60	15.20	953.35	8.8.60	10.15	1106.40	5.12.60	6.00	1279.45	10.3.61	9.15	1394.30
17.12.59	11.65	763.10	19.4.60	8.05	961.40	10.8.60	9.30	1116.10	6.12.60	8.30	1288.15	21.3.61	10.05	1404.35
30.12.59	3.10	766.20	20.4.60	7.20	969.00	8.9.60	23.30	1139.40	8.12.60	8.30	1296.45	23.3.61	8.20	1412.55
31.12.59		769.50	21.4.60	9.15	978.15	12.9.60	9.10	1139.10	12.12.60	8.35	1304.50	27.3.61	8.05	1421.00
5.1.59	6.10	772.30	22.4.60	15.20	993.35	14.9.60	9.30	1148.40	13.12.60	1.05	1305.55	6.4.61	10.00	1431.00

130

977 Major Secu 5858 Hrs.

SECTION C — GENERAL DATA AND SPECIAL EQUIPMENT FITTED

ASSEMBLY	DATA		ASSEMBLY	DATA	ASSEMBLY	DATA
GEARBOX S/N	FITTED HOURS	DATE				
No1. 35917	5858	11/69				
No2 62493	6161	4/8/70				
No3 65416	5858	11/69				
No4 62613	5858	11/69				
X DRIVE						
1. A/62/6251	5858	11/69				
2. DRG/1358/64	6161	4/8/70				
3. DRG/214/64	5858	11/69				
4. DRG/1232/67	5858	11/69				

SECTION E — MAJOR COMPONENT CHANGES AND MAJOR REPAIRS

DATE	Hours Flown		DATE	Hours Flown	
12.5.69	5273	NOSE w/c S/N ACCU/57/70/(37) FITTED due change at 9273 A/F HRS. TYPE 20009 O/004	5.12.69	5858	Pt + STBD JETTISON VALVES CHANGED
			"		Pt + STBD FUEL VENT VALVES CHANGED.
5/12/69	5858	NOSE w/c RETRACTING STAY S/N DRG 46/10/63 FITTED.	"		Pt + STBD PNEUMATIC VALVES CHANGED
"		MAIN w/c Pt + STBD DOWN LOCK JACKS FITTED.	"		AILERON SERVO MOTOR S/N A555/58 FITTED.
"		MAIN w/c UP. LOCK JACK FITTED	"		RUDDER SERVO MOTOR S/N C350/58 FITTED.
"		Pt. MAIN w/c RADIUS ROD S/N EHLW/188/37 FITTED. (NIL HOURS)	"		ELEVATOR SERVO MOTOR S/N D120/58 FITTED.
"		STBD MAIN w/c RADIUS ROD SERIAL No. EHLW/188/42 FITTED (NIL HOURS)	"		STBD ELECTROMATIC VALVE S/N S5116 FITTED
"		Pt + STBD ELECTRO PNEUMATIC VALVE S/N. D27521 + 256 FITTED	"		Pt. ELECTROMATIC VALVE CHANGED S/N 237 Ft.
"		ALL FLAME SWITCHES CHANGED	"		Pt. MAIN w/c S/N EHL 47M FITTED
			"		STBD MAIN w/c S/N. EHL 47M 57 FITTED
			15.3.70	5896	STBD ELECTROMATIC VALVE CHANGED
			2.3.70	5885	STBD DOWN LOCK JACK CHANGED
			10.4.70	5953	STBD VIPER EL/VALVE 37VA/6766 CHANGED
			10.6.70	6087	STBD VIPER EL/VALVE S/N 238 FITTED.
			10.6.70	6087	STBD VIPER ELECTROMATIC TAP S/N 7 FITTED.

AIRCRAFT No. WR 977 TYPE SHACKLETON MARK 3 PH3 AIRFRAME RECORD SERIAL No. 2 (TJ0) R.A.F. FORM 4001 Revised Aug. 1953

SECTION A — TRANSFER DETAILS

TRANSFER DATE	AUTHORITY	UNIT TO	HOURS FLOWN	TRANSFER DATE	AUTHORITY	UNIT TO	HOURS FLOWN

SECTION B — INSTALLATION DETAILS OF ENGINES, ENGINE CHANGE UNITS, POWER PLANTS & PROPELLERS

ITEM	POS.	INITIAL INSTALLATION R.A.F. Serial No.	A/F Hrs.	1st CHANGE R.A.F. Serial No.	A/F Hrs.	2nd CHANGE R.A.F. Serial No.	A/F Hrs.	3rd CHANGE R.A.F. Serial No.	A/F Hrs.	4th CHANGE R.A.F. Serial No.	A/F Hrs.
ENGINE	1	44423A641007	5675								
"	2	44181A638243	5485	43343A628740	5896	44031A633043	6033	43824A628816	6034	44023A688440	6087
"	3	43579A621533	5185.43	44157A639249	5283.30	44076A638135	5853				
"	4	44295A640809	5655	44074A639094	6161						
P. PLANT	1	155755	5675								
"	2	155640	5485	155704	5896	155768	6033	163634	6064	160657	6087
"	3	161704	5185.43	160657	5283.30	162519	5853				
"	4	160613	5655	160700	6161						

Examples of WR977's record cards and flight logs from which much of the data has been transposed.

Water Methanol Take-Off Due.

Prop. Feathering Functional Due.

The sortie details are unknown, but she took-off with Water-Methanol injection at 1300 hours. She was in the air for 7.45 hours., landing at 2045 hours. Each Viper was running for 37 minutes, 2.30 minutes of that at Maximum Power, and made two Viper-assisted take-offs. During the flight the pilot carried out air check on No.3 Engine, which was 'Satisfactory', as were the prop. feathering functionals. Water-Meth. check carried out, but the stall check was not.

29.06.71: Flt.Lt. Keith Jarvis accepted the aircraft from the C/T at 0800. On the flight a 'Stall Check, Due To Port Detector Unit Change' was required. Bryn Wayt was the Co-Pilot for this sortie, leaving the ground with Viper assistance at 1040 hours for an L.R.O.F.E. and Airborne SAR cover for Prince William of Gloucester. Bryn Wayt notes on this flight:

> Airborne SAR - Looks like we are 'mother' to Prince William of Gloucester today. Whilst airborne for 9 hrs and 15 mins we carry out routine recce/sub hunting filling in time.

They landed at 1955 hours after flying for 9.15 hours, 5.10 hours of which had been flown by Keith Jarvis and the remainder by Flt.Lt. Wayt. The Port Viper had been running for 25 minutes, with one minute at Max., the STBD. for 24.15 minutes with 1.20 mins. at Max. power. They did not carry out a stall check, and 3 defects were noted at the end of the flight although no details are given.

30.06.71: At 0545 hours the aircraft Captain (unknown) signed the acceptance certificate, also signed by a Sgt. Ground Engineer. A Stall Warning check was required as it hadn't yet been carried out since the Detector Unit change.

She took-off at 0745 hours, apparently without Vipers, but each was run for 27 minutes during the sortie, with 1.15 minutes of that at Maximum Power. The sortie lasted 7.55 hours., she landed at 1540 hours. No Stall Warning Check was made. However a note made by the Captain says: 'Stickshakers in until 145 Knots, on TO and in at 150 Knots in level flight.'

31.05.71: 2 Stbd. Trim tabs and port tip tank changed at 6495 airframe hours.

06.07.71: This was the same entry in the F.700 as the previous flight, no new date or signatures. She took to the air at 1405 hours. and flew for 5.45 hours., landing again at 1950 hours. Each Viper ran for 46 minutes, including 1.15 mins. at full power during the flight.

07.07.71: No Flight. RLE's state: Viper L.P. Cock Support Bracket (PT. M/P) Temporarily Secured. She Was Serviceable To Fly Until Next Primary Service When A Permanent Repair Will Be Made. Authorised by Sqdn.Ldr. Morgan.

08.07.71: The C/T signed the certificate of acceptance at 1330 hours, and she was accepted by the Captain Flt.Lt. Phil Zarraga, subject to the following conditions: Stall Warning Check required, Check Nosewheel Red On Throttle Settings.
    She did not fly as No.4 Rear Prop. was changed at 6564.20 hrs.

12.07.71: Flt.Lt. Phil Zarraga accepted WR 977 at 1140 hours with No Tip Tank Facility, and the same checks required as for the previous date. He took off with Flt.Lt. David Ladbrooke as Co-Pilot at 1300 hours for a Reconnaissance in the Mediterranean, of 10.05 hours. landing at 2305 hours. They made only the one Viper Take-off, and in flight the Port was run for 28 minutes in total, with 1.25 minutes at Max. power, and the Starboard for 40 minutes with the same time at maximum power. 4 Defects were noted. Flt.Lt. Zarraga carried out the Stall Warning check and Throttle Red check, both were 'Satisfactory'.

12. - 14.07.71: No.1 T.U. Change.

14.07.71: Phil Zarraga accepted WR977 at again, still with no tip tank facility and subject to RLE'S, he made two flights on this date, the first was a Training sortie, taking off at 1555 hours and landing at 2155 hours after 6 hours flying. David Ladbrooke was again the Co-Pilot.
    The second sortie began at 2155 hours for more training, this time

though Flt.Lt. Zarraga was Co-Pilot to Sqdn.Ldr. Ken Appleford for more training lasting 2.05 hours. landing at 2400 hours. In total they made three Viper assisted take-offs, three landings and 5 rollers. Each Viper ran for 1.41 hours., at full power the Port ran for 13.05 mins. and 11.15 mins. for the Starboard. Phil Zarraga recalls that without Vipers and with a full fuel load, the Griffon Engines would be running at full power until fuel weight reduced sufficiently to reduce power. However, he tells that with Vipers one could be kept running and could reduce the Griffon power under those conditions by about 400 RPM, perhaps from 2600 to 2400 RPM. Seven defects were noted during this flight.

19.07.71: Sqdn.Ldr. John Arnaud accepted '977 at 1430 hours still with no tip tank facility, and with the 'Nitrogen Master Cock Turned Off', and subject to RLE's. They left the ground at 1550 hours apparently without Viper assistance for a 7.40 hour. undetailed sortie landing at 2330 hours.

Viper running times were:

PORT	-	2.09 hrs.	inc. 9 mins. at Max.
STBD	-	2.10 hrs.	inc. 9 mins. at Max.

She made 3 landings and 4 rollers.

20.07.71: Sqdn.Ldr. Arnaud again accepted 'Bravo' at 0500 hours, still without tip tank facility and with the Nitrogen Master Cock off. She was 'S' to fly subject to RLE's. The RLE's note an 'Out Of Phase Compass Swing Required' and an extension to Primary Service granted. She left the ground with Vipers running at 0655 hours landing at 0920 hours after the undetailed 2.25 hour. sortie. Each Viper had been run for 1.13 hours. with 1 min. at Max. Sqdn.Ldr. Arnaud notes after the flight that everything was 'Satisfactory' indicating that 'No Defects Are Observed Or Reported.'

21.07.71: Sqdn.Ldr. Arnaud again accepted WR977 (time unknown) and took her off at 1445 hours for an undetailed sortie. The length of the sortie at 2.50 hours. suggests it was a Crew Training or Mandatory sortie of some kind. He landed again at 1735 hours. There is no note of the lack of a tip tank facility obviously indicating rectification. He made only one Viper take-off, with 14 minutes running for each, including 1 min. at full power. It would seem that some defects were noted.

21. - 26.07.71: Grounded due to fitment of a recon No.1 Griffon engine, which had run for 511 hours total. This was the last Griffon change she underwent.

26.07.71: Notes affecting use:
A/C Serviceable to fly subject to RLE's.
Air Test on No.1 Engine.
Air Compass Swing after Engine change.
At 0915 hours she was signed for by Sqdn.Ldr. Arnaud, and left the ground with Water Methanol Injection at 0955 hours for the necessary airtest, landing 25 minutes later. Each Viper was running for 27 minutes, but no take-off with them is noted, even though running for that long it would suggest so. He made one landing and one roller. In the After Flight Certificate he notes: 'Air Swing Carried Out, Water/Meth. carried out. Air check on No.1 Engine. Satis.'

29.07.71: Primary Service due at 26.07.71, extended for 17 days until August 12th. Also around this time No.4 TU was changed.

29.07.71: Flt.Lt. Whitome signed for her as fit to fly subject to RLE's. She left the runway with Vipers at 1625 hours, with 'Dicky' Henderson as his Engineer who notes the flight, hist last in '977, as a CASEX C2, which lasted 4 hours Day and 5.15 hours Night. They landed her at 0140 hours. Viper running times are not available having been improperly entered.

29.07 - 03.08.71: Stbd. Viper changed at 6605 airframe hours, her last engine change of all. Fitted on August 4th. A note in the F700's gives details of the Viper's life and use.

05.08.71: Last RLE entry: 'Port Mainplane No.3 Aileron Shroud Panel Hinge Cracked'. The rectification section notes 'A/C Fit To Fly Subject To Inspection Every 7 Days.' Authorised by Sqdn.Ldr. Morgan.

10.08.71: Flt.Lt. H.P. Zarraga was the Pilot for this sortie, but he did not sign for 'Bravo'. Obviously one of his crew members (Capt. for the flight) who signed for her at 0800 hours. She was due for a Prop. Feathering Functionals and a Compass Air Swing, and was fit to fly subject to RLE's.

Flt.Lt.'s Zarraga and Ladbrooke took to the air for a 10 hour Recce in the Mediterranean, landing at 2000 hours. They carried out the Compass Swing and Prop. Functionals, both of which were 'Satisfactory'. Each Viper was run for 2.15 mins. at Maximum Power and 36 minutes in total. 3 defects were found, unknown.

12.08.71: At 0830 hours WR977 was accepted by the same crew member as the previous day. The pilot was Flt.Lt. Zarraga with John Aldington as his Co-Pilot. They took her off at 1025 hours for an 8.30 hour Med. Recce touching down at 1855 hours. They made two landings and two Viper assisted take-offs. The Viper running times were, Port 54 mins. with Max. for 2.45 mins., and Stbd. 1.02 hours. inc. 2.45 mins. Max.

She was prepared for a flight on a date following this which was not noted, but she was not flown. Perhaps this was due to a No.2 Rear Prop. change at 6623 airframe hours. She did not fly for nearly a week.

19.08.71: Conditions affecting use of aircraft:
Stall Warning System Air Check Req'd.
A/C Fit To Fly Subject to RLE's.

The certificate was prepared at 0845 hours and she was accepted by the Squadron OC Wing Commander Bowyer. Bryn Wayt, his Co-Pilot for this sortie notes him as 'Son of the family firm, 'Bowyer' famous for it's pork pies, etc.' They took-off, Viper assisted of course, at 1000 hours, for a sortie which Flt.Lt. Wayt notes as an L.R.O.F.E./OPS flight, lasting 6 hours., all flown by the OC. He notes:

> No.2 Eng shut down. Due to overheating. The Squadron Commander was on board - Wg Cdr Bowyer. *Another* three-engine landing.

They landed at 1600 hours, they did carry out a Stall Warning check, and Wg.Cdr. Bowyer noted the 'Incident Report' of the Engine Overheating. They made a 'PAN CALL' which Flt.Lt. Wayt notes as 2nd highest emergency before a Mayday. Each Viper ran at full power for 1.30 mins., the total time for the Stbd. being 1.21.20 hours., the Port for 30.10 mins. No rectification is recorded.

23.08.71: The conditions affecting use was completed by a C/T at 1540 hours, Stall Warning Check was still needed. Flt.Lt. Phil Zarraga signed for '977 for the last time, and made a Viper Take-Off at 1620 hours for a 2.25 hour. flight to Sigonella with his Co-Pilot David Ladbrooke, landing again at 1845 hours. There is no note of whether they returned from Sigonella, or not. It can only be assumed that they did and this was included in the entry, they made two Viper Take-Offs and two landings. Each Viper was run for an hour, including 2.20 mins. at Max. This was Flt.Lt. Zarraga's last flight in 'Bravo', he'd flown her for 103.55 hours. in total.

26.08.71: Acceptance certificate was filled in at 1300 hours, the only conditions affecting her operation being 'Subject to RLE's' and a Stall Warning check still being needed. She was accepted by Wg.Cdr. Bowyer. He took off at 1415 hours for an undetailed 5.55 hours. touching down again at 2010 hours. The Vipers were run for 2.38 hours. in total. 12 defects were found during the flight and he made two landings and two rollers.

02.09.71: Obviously after rectification of defects found, she was ready for flight, with a Water Methanol take-off due, at 1300 hours, she was accepted by the OC for a 2.10 hour. flight taking off at 1500 hours and landing at 1710 hours. This would seem to be Mandatory flying or OT of some kind as 2 landings, 3 rollers, and consequently 5 Viper take-offs were made, one of which was Water Methanol injected.

Each Viper ran for 5.20 mins. at Max. Power, and in total they ran for 3.52.20 hours. Six defects were noted during the flight.

07.09.71: A Water Methanol was due, and a Taxi Test was required. The Serviceability Certificate filled in at 1230 hours, being accepted by Flt.Lt. Bryn Wayt, for OT, Mandatory and OP.S taking off at 1425 hours, but was re-called after 4 hours Day and 1 hour Night, with Flt.Lt. Wight-Boycott as Co-Pilot. They also completed 1 hour. 'Simulated' and 'Actual' Instrument flying, and a GCA and PAR. Flt.Lt. Wayt carried out the taxi test which was 'Satisfactory', and 2 Viper take-offs, 3 landings & 4 rollers.

Total running time for the Port Viper was 1.06.25 hours., and 1.06 hours. for the Stbd., with 2 mins. at Max. Defects were noted during the sortie.

137

17.09.71: The Serviceability Log was filled in at 1115 hours. and all that was required was a Prop. Feathering Functionals check. She was accepted by the 1st and 2nd Pilots jointly, the reason becoming evident, both Wg.Cdr. Bowyer and Flt.Lt. Wayt signed for her, the latter being the Crew Captain. Two flights were made, the first at 1150 hours for OT, a Stage II Exercise, and a Trial, flying for 3.45 hours with the OC at the controls, including 30 mins. on instruments. They landed at Sigonella.

The second flight was the return to Luqa, flown by Flt.Lt. Wayt with Sqdn.Ldr. Arnaud in the right-hand seat. They left the runway at Sigonella at 1535 hours and landed back at Luqa 50 minutes later. The total for the day was 4.35 hours., each Viper being on Max. power for 4.50 mins. and in total the Prt ran for 1.23.10 hours. and the Stbd. 2.03.45 hours. She made 3 Viper take-offs and 3 landings. 5 Defects were found during the flight.

22.09.71: Serviceability Log: Filled in at 1200 hours
1. Prop. Feathering Functional due.
2. A/C 'S' To Fly Subject To RLE's.
3. Air Check Req'd. On Scanner For Correct Function To Attack From 1st & 2nd Position.

Flt.Lt. Whitome signed for '977 but no details are recorded, she seems to have been away with the Crew. The Daily Flying Times Log shows that she did fly for 1.40 hours.

23.09.71: A note which confirms that she was away - 'TIMES & HRS. B/F FROM TRAVELLER', this indicates the travelling log would contain the details. On this date she is recorded in the DFT Log as flying for 7.35 hours. and then for 1.50 hours. 3 Viper take-offs were made, and had been run for a total of around 4 hours.

24.09.71: Not Flown. Although she was prepared for a flight and the F.700 was prepared.

30.09.71: Serviceability Log was filled in at 0800 hours, she was fit to fly 'Subject To RLE's' and a 'Stall Warning Check Req'd'.

She was accepted by Sqdn.Ldr. Ken Appleford for an 8.50 hour flight, leaving the runway at 1100 hours and touching down at 2000 hours. He carried out the Stall Warning checks which were 'Satisfactory'. He made one landing, one roller, and two Viper assisted take-offs. The Port Viper was run for 25 minutes, the Stbd. for 24.

07.10.71: She was accepted at 0830 hours by Sqdn.Ldr. Appleford again. A Water Methanol take-off was due. He took her off with Water Meth. boost at 0955 hours, flew her for 10.10 hours, and landed again at 2005 hours. The Water Methanol T/O was 'Satisfactory'.

Port Viper ran for 41 mins (2.20 mins. at Max.), Stbd. Viper ran for 31 mins. (2.20 mins. at Max.).

18

WR977's Last Operational Flights and Her Last Flight of All.

12.10.71: She was accepted by Flt.Lt. Bryn Wayt at 1500 hours as fit to fly 'Subject To RLE's'. Flt.Lt. Ted Buddin was his Co-Pilot for a Mandatory sortie, taking to the air at 1615 hours, and completed 2 landings and 5 rollers, 4 of these were flapless touch-downs. They landed at 1800 hours, the last 5 mins. of the sortie was at night, and lasted 1.45 hours. Eight Viper Take-offs were made, and the running times were, Port 1.31.20 hours. and the Stbd. 1.30.40 hours., each with 4.18 mins. at Max.

14.10.71: Flt.Lt. Bryn Wayt accepted WR977 for what was to be her last operational sortie with Flt.Lt. Buddin as his Co-Pilot, at 0845 hours for OT, Stage II, and Skid Bombing, South of Sicilly and Close Support Training. She took off at 0955 hours for her last operational sortie and her last flight for a month. Flight duration was 6.10 hours, landing at 1605 hours. Flt.Lt. Wayt completed 1.30 hours of Instrument flying ('Simulated'). Only one Viper take-off was made, and Viper running times were:

Port 30.50 mins.,   3.40 mins. at Max.
Stbd. 30.20 mins.,   3.40 mins. at Max.

This was Flt.Lt. Wayt's last flight with WR977, he'd flown 72.45 hours. in her and notes:

My last flight with her. From August until today, she gave me no more trouble, and we parted good griends.

27.10.71: Special Weapons Check carried out. Satisfactory.

29.10.71: From now until she left service, only the various levels and certain systems were checked, and some photographic equipment was removed, the run down of '977 ready for retirement had begun in earnest.

06.11.71: No flight. Last re-fuelling, 770 Gallons, bringing the fuel load to 4120 Gallons.

0900: De-icing fluid for windscreen and aerofoil, and oxygen levels were checked. No extra was necessary.

0930: Oil, Coolant and Water Methanol levels were checked. No extra was necessary.

07.11.71: By 0700 hours Before Flight Certificate was signed as 'Essential Services' which obviously referred to the serviceability of all that was necessary for the ferry flight back to the UK. The pneumatic and Nitrogen systems having been checked. At 0800 hours the pyrotechnics installed were checked. She only carried emergency flares or 'Signal Cartridges' necessary for the ferry flight. She carried 6 x 1½" Reds, 6 x 1½" Yellows, and 12 x 1½" Greens. Ballast weights were fitted, as the guns weren't. She was prepared to be signed over at 0700, but the certificate was re-signed at 1200 hours and accepted by Sqdn.Ldr. John Arnaud, who flew with Flt.Lt. Ted Buddin as his Co-Pilot. It was a 6.25 hour transit back to the UK, landing at St. Mawgan. Her fate initially was fire fighting practise at RAF Thorney island. However that was changed and she was to be fired at Finningley, Yorkshire.

09.11.71: Flt.Lt. Ted Buddin was the 1st Pilot the last time '977 took to the air to fly to Finningley, a 2.40 hour transit. Ted Buddin notes:

> This was the final delivery to UK before Dom Mintoff kicked us off the island. I remember No.3 (?) engine playing up badly on the approach to land (making loud banging noises with fluctuations in boost and RPM) - glad to get it on the ground! We believed at the time the aircraft was to be a fire practise machine at Finningley!

WR977 obviously knew her fate and managed to resist: escaping destruction is something she is noted for, right through her life. Ted Buddin had flown 47.30 hours. in '977.

In fact, she was chosen to become part of the 'Finningly Air Museum' and be used as a static exhibit at air shows.
Even though some MR.3 Shack's served until the next year, they were newer than '977 and she retired as the longest serving MR.3 with the Royal Air Force having completed 14 years and 1 month total, and 11 years 6 months if Phase mods are excluded. She flew a recorded total of almost 6700 airframe hours (6696.45) although the actual total was

slightly more taking it up to around 6800 or more.

So far her life had been very interesting taking part in many of the more interesting events which occurred in the period 1957 - 71 as well as her fair share of the arduous and dirty tasks the Shackleton was called on to perform. She had so far escaped fire fighting allotments twice, and the rest of her life was to prove intriguing also. At some point at the end of her life an Engineer had scrawled on her Engineer's panel something which sums it all up, **'Shacks are wonderful, in their own way'.**

APPENDIX 1

GLOSSARY OF TERMS

AIR TEST - Flight carried out to check an aircraft system or systems after repair, replacement, service, or modification.

AIRWAYS EXERCISE - The aircraft flies specified airway routes.

ASSYMETRIC - Flying with one (or more) engine(s) shut down on one side.

AUTOLYCUS - Submarine detection equipment which can pick up any change of ionisation in the air caused by a submarine diesel exhaust. Also known as 'Sniffer'. Distinguishable by large sensor on forward section of port fuselage above bomb door.

B/F - Brought Forward.

BOMBING - Tthis is usually practice for bombing submarines, with the weapons being dropped on either a Radar Buoy or a submarine simulation target towed by a motor launch usually referred to as a 'Skid'.

CASEX - Combined Anti-Submarine Exercise - Carried out in conjunction with Royal Navy Ships or Submarines. No.'s such as 31, 35 or 41 refer to the specific details of the exercise. Each one was very precise being carried out at a specific time and in specific area with the exercising ship or sub. They would carry out pre-designated manoeuvres in order that each crew member could practise his operational detection tasks.

CAT. CHECK - A flight on which members of the Coastal Command Categorisation Board assess the skills of the crew. (See Sqdn.Ldr. Denham's notes on this, 4th June 1970).

CLOSE SUPPORT - (Of Escort Shipping Convoys) - When an aircraft on anti-submarine patrol around a group of ships e.g. Task Force or

Convoy, is controlled by a ship in the group. Also Distant support, again overseeing safe movement of shipping.

CODING - Most radio communications transmitted to and from a Maritime aircraft were coded for security.

CONTINUATION TRAINING - A flying exercise including Circuits and Bumps and practising those conditions that do not normally occur during routine flights e.g. Flapless and assymetric landings.

CREEPING LINE AHEAD (CLA) - The aircraft is flown on a creeping search pattern (one of several used) during Search and Rescue or looking for a submarine.

CSU - Constant Speed Unit.

C/T - Chief Technician (Groundcrew Rank).

DC - Depth Charge.

DI-STAFF - Directing Staff officially appointed to oversee correct execution of an exercise such as JASSEX.

ECM - Electronic Counter Measures - A system used for detection and jamming of radio/radar signals in this case from a submarine. The system used on the Shackleton was called 'Orange Harvest' and is distinguishable on post-Phase 2 aircraft by a large plinth on the top centre of the fuselage which often occupied with a large 'Spark Plug' shaped aerial.

GCA - Ground Controlled Approach - The Air Traffic Control talk an aircraft down on to the runway by using radar and enable the aircraft to land safely in bad weather.

ILS - Instrument Landing System - A precise and accurate system for guiding a pilot onto the runway in poor visibility. Often practised to ensure correct technique can be employed when necessary.

IRT - Instrument Rating Test - A check carried out on a pilot's ability to fly an aircraft purely on instruments, each pilot is given a colour code according to his standard, a standard which has to be maintained and can be improved upon up to the highest code of 'Master Green'.

Lindholme Gear - Survival gear carried in Bomb or Stores bay of a Shackleton which can be dropped in case of emergency to those in danger in the sea. It contained a dinghy and food etc., to ensure their well being. Three canisters are joined together with 600 yards of buoyant rope.

LP COCK - Low Pressure fuel valve in engine.

L.R.O.F.E. - (Long Range) Operational Flying Exercise - An exercise concentrating on the operational aspects such as bombing, Sonics, Gunnery, etc.

MANDATORY (TRAINING) - Often referred to simply as 'Mandatory' this was the minimum requirement for the amount of flying a pilot must carry out in a month to keep up-to-date. 'Circuits and bumps' or 'rollers' with or without flaps, and with an engine shut down etc. were carried out, ILS Approaches, etc.

MHQ - Maritime Head Quarters.

Mod.(s) - Modifications - Improvements carried out to an aircraft during it's life.

M/P - Main plane.

NAVEX - Navigation Exercise - A set Navigation Exercise but with other exercises being carried out on an opportunity basis, e.g. Radar Homings. Carried out between 500 and 1500 feet. No Aids refers to method of navigation in this case pure navigation without use of aircraft aids. This had to be practised in case the aircraft system failed.

NDB - Non-Directional Beacon - Beacons which provide the aircraft with signals which give bearings and can be used as an ILS system but is less accurate.

OT - Operational Training

PAR - Further blind landing guidance system.

PHOTOGRAPHY - Hand held cameras were used to photograph subjects from observation positions within the aircraft. Fixed cameras (retractable) on the underside of the aircraft used to assess attacks or identify illuminated targets at night.

RADAR HOMINGS - Pilot guided to target by operator using aircraft radar.

RECCE - Reconnaissance.

ROLLER - Also referred to as circuits and bumps where the aircraft touches down on the runway with mainwheels and lifts off again.

RTB - Return To Base usually caused by aircraft fault, etc.

SAR - Search And Rescue.

SARAH - Search And Rescue And Homing - Equipment for SAR, detects signals and homes the aircraft in to survivors. (Prior to Phase 2)

SARBE - Search and Rescue Beacon - Improved SARAH system basically fitted at Phase 2.

SHADEX - Shadowing Exercise - practising shaddowing a hostile ship where the aircraft monitors it's movements from well out of sight or detection.

SIMTEX - See Stage II largely the same exercise.

SNORT SIM. - Simulation of a 'snorting' submarine for the aircraft to detect and prosecute an attack.

STAGE II - 'An airborne anti-submarine exercise using a round based simulator unit transmitting a 'live' submarine underwater accoustic contact information/data.'

SURVEX - Surveillance Exercise.

TAC-EX - Tactical Exercise.

TAC-NAV - Tactical Navigation.

TORPEX - See Mike Head's explanation 1st May 64.

TU - Translation Unit - Part of Prop. Contra-rotation system.

U/S - Unserviceable.

W/OP - Wireless Operator.

Wx - Weather

APPENDIX 2

WR977'S KNOWN OPERATING LOCATIONS

United Kingdom
RAF Aldergrove, Northern Ireland
RAF Ballykelly, Northern Ireland
Bitteswell, Leicestershire (Hawker Siddeley Aviation)
RAF Bovingdon, Hertfordshire
Chadderton, Manchester (AVRO)
RNAS Culdrose, Cornwall
Farnborough, Hampshire (Royal Aircraft Establishment)
Glasgow, Renfrew, Scotland
Langar, Nottinghamshire (AVRO)
RAF Leuchars, Fife, Scotland
RAF Lossiemouth, Morayshire, Scotland
RAF Kinloss, Morayshire, Scotland
RAF Manston, Kent
RAF Machrihanish, Kintyre, Scotland
RAF Marham, Norfolk
RAF St.Eval, Cornwall
RAF St. Mawgan, Cornwall
RAF Thorney Island, Hampshire
RAF Turnhouse, Lothian, Scotland
Wallasey, Merseyside
RAF Wittering, Cambridgeshire
Woodford, Manchester (AVRO)

Europe
Aalborg, Denmark
RAF Akrotiri, Cyprus
Bodo, Norway
Decimomannu, Sicilly
Espinho/Ovar, Portugal

RAF Gibraltar, Gibraltar
RAF Hal Far, Malta
Lajes, Azores
Lisbon, Portugal
Lann Bihoue, France
RAF Luga, Malta
Naples, Italy
RAF Nicosia, Cyprus
Oerland, Norway
Sigonella, Italy

Africa

Cape Town, South Africa
El Adem, North Africa
Embakasi, Kenya
Entebbe, Uganda
Kano, Nigeria
Khormakser, Aden, Yemen
Majunga, Madagascar
Nairobi, Kenya
Salisbury, Rhodesia (Zimbabwe)
USAF Wheelus, Tripoli, Libya

Americas

Brunswick, Maine, USA
Curacao, Dutch Antilles
USAF Kindley, Bermuda
Maiquetia, Venezuela

Asia Pacific

RAF Butterworth, Malaysia
RAF Changi, Singapore
RAF Gan, The Maldives, Indian Ocean

BIBLIOGRAPHY

ASHWORTH, C.
Avro Shackleton MR.Mk.3. Alan W. Hall (Publications).

ASHWORTH, R.C.B.
Avro's Maritime Heavyweight - The Shackleton. Aston Publications.

HOWARD, P.J.
Profile 243 - Avro Shackleton Mks. 1 - 4. Profile Publications.